PREPPY STYLE

PREPPY STYLE

A MODERN GUIDE TO TIMELESS FASHION

ROSALYN GOMERSALL

ROCK
POINT

3

Prep
Icons

52

4

Prep
Essentials

98

Introduction

A Timeless Style

Preppy is timeless. It's one of the most popular trends in the history of trends, so much so, it's now considered to be "trendless"—a style that comes and goes and also never leaves. It's composed of fashion staples you can come back to time and again. You undoubtedly know the ones: polo shirts, chinos, navy blazers, cable-knit sweaters and the like, often featuring classic patterns like checks and stripes.

Preppy—often used interchangeably with "Ivy"—takes its name from the private "prep" schools that affluent, well-connected and, in all likelihood, white students usually attended before going to Ivy League universities, which is where the distinctive dress code developed. The relaxed, lived-in, and leisurely cool attire was a way of signaling wealth and social status without ostentation. Fashion was a visual language that said, "I have money, but I don't care to flaunt it." As preppy style spread from the campuses of the elite into the mainstream, it became more than just clothing; it was an aspirational lifestyle. Prep went from being the hallmark of upper-class exclusivity to being a cultural, worldwide phenomenon—embraced by everyone from Black jazz musicians to Japanese hipsters.

In the 1980s, *The Official Preppy Handbook* played a significant role in this shift, offering a satirical guide to adopting the preppy look. This coincided with the rise of Ralph Lauren and the launch of J.Crew, with both brands helping to solidify prep's staying power. Whether known under different names by a new generation—"old money," "stealth wealth," and even "quiet luxury"—reinterpreted with different silhouettes, details, and proportions, preppy's appeal continues to last in the decades since. That's the thing with prep: it has a unique ability to adapt and evolve with the times. It's the reason preppy style isn't going anywhere, and why it will always be reinvented and reimagined.

1

The Origins of Prep

Preppy style, once seen as an exclusive signifier of old-money status, has become ubiquitous. Pare back any American trend, or even brand, and you'll find prep at its roots.

O ne mention of prep and it's easy to assemble the preppy look in your mind's eye: a cream, cable-knit, three-ply cashmere sweater draped over the shoulders and tied loosely at the front; Nantucket red chinos paired with Weejuns (no socks, of course); and if we're talking about the home—a wingback chair with a Bloody Mary placed on a mahogany side table. It can even conjure up a whole lifestyle; playing the eleventh hole of the Maidstone in East Hampton, enjoying a martini, or two, at the Edgartown yacht club on Martha's Vineyard, or dining on fresh New England clambakes in Maine.

Preppy wasn't a style that appeared suddenly. It has developed over time—so, where did it all begin? Lisa Birnbach's seminal book, *The Official Preppy Handbook*, states that "looking, acting and ultimately being Prep is not restricted to an elite minority," yet the first to don the style was exactly that: white, Anglo-Saxon protestants—otherwise known as WASPs. These were well-off young men—almost exclusively boys at the time—who attended prestigious British preparatory schools (hence the name). From striped blazers to V-neck sweaters, preppy style grew out of these British school uniforms.

It wasn't until the 1880s that private prep schools, along with preppy style, crossed the Atlantic into American culture. Unlike in Britain, American prep schools did not gradually evolve into leading institutions. For the Americans, they symbolized class and upper-class privilege from their very beginnings and served to "prepare" students for Ivy League universities. Students offered a spot in the Ivy League came from old WASP families that dominated the wealthy social circles, and in those days for the schools, this often outweighed being brilliant or hardworking. Instead, students competed for entrance into the prestigious social clubs: Skull and Bones at Yale, Ivy at Princeton, the Porcellian at Harvard, etc. For the select few, these clubs offered invaluable connections, paving the way to influential positions in law firms, banks, the State Department, and, for some alumni (like George W. Bush and Theodore Roosevelt), even the White House.

The athletic pursuits of Ivy League students, such as equestrian, sailing, tennis, and golf, combined with influences from British sports—rowing, cricket, polo, and tennis—further influenced the preppy aesthetic. Elements of these classic sports kits became so ingrained in daily life that students would wear them from the boathouse to class and even to dinner. At a time when formal attire was worn almost everywhere, preppy offered a more relaxed alternative and laid the groundwork as one of the earliest forms of athleisure. As fashion designer Tommy Hilfiger so deftly put it: "Preppy style has its roots in England, but the English version is staid and serious. The American version is irreverent. There should always be a twist."

Equestrian Influence and Inspiration

Horse riding has been a popular pastime among the wealthy and elite since the sixteenth and seventeenth centuries, and it wasn't long before tailored riding gear started to shape everyday fashion. The high-quality materials used such as wool and leather were not only practical but they also produced long-lasting pieces of clothing. Today, riding boots have turned into heeled booties, riding coats are now blazers, and leather pants and jackets have become statement pieces only a select few can pull off. The timeless pieces and associations with sophistication and elegance have continued to elevate wardrobes and are most often created by luxurious brands such as Hermès, Gucci, and Burberry.

Brooks Brothers

A fresh twist was exactly what Henry Sands Brooks offered when he founded H. & D.H. Brooks & Co. in 1818 New York City. He changed the menswear game forever by rejecting the rigid, custom-made silhouettes of the Victorian era in favor of something much more relaxed. Adopting the philosophy of "makers and merchants in one," Brooks—alongside his four sons—took full control over every aspect of production to make sure the brand's pieces were of the highest quality.

After Henry Sands Brooks died in 1833, his sons took the helm and changed the name to Brooks Brothers. It is now the oldest continuously operating maker of menswear in America, and one that's been a part of almost every era-defining event in the country's history. Abraham Lincoln had on a signature Brooks Brothers black overcoat at the time of his assassination (as did JFK). Barack Obama donned his own on Inauguration Day. Clark Gable was married in it. There was an organized riot named after the brand in 2000 to stymie the Florida recount. Even the costumes in Baz Luhrmann's 2013 *The Great Gatsby* reimagining were all Brooks Brothers. As the first choice for all but four US presidents, of statesmen and countless other stars, who better to dress the privileged preps?

In F. Scott Fitzgerald's *This Side of Paradise*, many references to Brooks Brothers were made and would become a great sponsor for the company and its customers of college men across the United States. Inspired by the classic sporting silhouettes and casually tailored pieces imported from British prep schools, the brand created many of the iconic styles favored by Ivy Leaguers: the No. 1 Sack Suit, the Oxford-cloth button-down, and the striped repp tie to name a few.

They were also one of the first to introduce the seersucker suit, but it didn't initially do well and wouldn't become popular until another thirty years or so. Not only did Brooks Brothers invent and perfect these pieces, as early as the 1900s, the company was the go-to for what would eventually become the prep staples we know today.

A Big-City Style

New York was a big port, which meant everyone was on the move. A suit that could be quickly—and easily—picked up was needed. To meet demand, forward-thinking Henry Sands Brooks introduced the ready-to-wear suit in 1849. It was a bold move that radically changed how Americans dressed, with standardized suit sizes making tailoring more accessible, affordable, and wearable for the masses. Pioneers of the California Gold Rush, keen to avoid the delays of custom tailoring, flocked to Brooks Brothers. The brand was praised by the editors of Carroll's 1859 *New York City Directory* as being "the first to embark on what is now a leading commercial pursuit." The brand's innovative approach didn't end there. In 1896, while attending a polo match in England, John E. Brooks, the founder's grandson, observed that players' collars were buttoned down to keep them from flapping in the wind. Feeling inspired, he introduced the idea to Brooks Brothers. And so the now-iconic Oxford button-down shirt—a design regarded as "the most imitated item in fashion history"—was born.

Fitzgerald's Amory Blaine

By the early twentieth century, Brooks Brothers's clothing was synonymous with elite boarding schools and Ivy League institutions. So much so, it earned itself several mentions in F. Scott Fitzgerald's 1920 semi-autobiographical novel, *This Side of Paradise*. Based around the character Amory Blaine and his social circle, the book was an insight into the burgeoning preppy mindset at Princeton in the 1910s. And who better to write about the college's privileged, upper-class youth culture than Fitzgerald, an old Princetonian himself? College dressing had turned into a competition, with classmates obsessing over details like "the color of their neckties and the roll of their coats." Amory Blaine's mother even told him to "go to Brooks' and get some really nice suits." Back in the day, this would have involved a visit to the flagship Madison Avenue store. On a day trip up from Princeton's New Jersey campus, they'd stock up on their famous button-down shirts and buy one of the brand's three-button black suits—perhaps to wear to an internship at Goldman Sachs.

As many more began to dip their toes into prep in the 1920s and '30s, films, magazines, and advertising started to publicize the preppy look. Brands like Brooks Brothers and J. Press, early champions of Ivy style, opened stores near prestigious institutions such as Princeton, Yale, and Harvard. College campuses were now central hubs for the development of a distinctive and refined look. As an *Apparel Arts* article stated in 1933, "The American University man is justly famed for representing, as a class, a high standard of excellence in impersonal appearance. Much of the secret of this distinction lies in the fact that the first thing the freshman learns is the importance of never looking 'dressed up,' while always looking well-dressed."

The growing preference for dressing down also brought with it rougher, more casual fabrics—flannel pants, brushed Shetland sweaters, and Harris Tweed jackets—which joined the roster of preppy staples. Bass Weejun penny loafers, launched by shoemaker G.H. Bass & Co. in 1936, became the shoe of choice on campus, at the vacation hot spot Palm Beach, and ultimately everywhere else.

Princeton and Codifying the Style

In the midst of the Great Depression, when only the fortunate few were still able to afford school, Ivy League campuses remained a breeding ground for preppy style. Young college men were now recognized as being among the nation's best dressed. Penny loafers, varsity sweaters, and Oxford shirts were all put together with the effortless confidence of true WASP privilege.

It was Princeton, more than any other Ivy League college, that's credited with shaping the preppy aesthetic during the interwar years. The rural New Jersey campus, surrounded by six hundred acres (243 ha) of farmland, was more isolated than its rivals Harvard and Yale. This, as well as having a particularly affluent student body, created an especially insular culture which meant fitting in was key.

Princetonians themselves established and upheld a well-defined social pecking order. For much of the first half of the century, Princeton freshmen and sophomores were traditionally banned from wearing certain clothing, including white flannel pants and striped ties. As a 1964 article from *The Daily Princetonian* confirmed, "freshmen wore a black turtleneck jersey and corduroy pants. When sophomores or upperclassmen approached, yearlings [or freshmen] were expected to get off the sidewalk until their elders had passed." Dressing like a true Princetonian was a privilege that had to be earned and reinforced the college's strict codes of social hierarchy and exclusivity through fashion. As athletics dominated Princeton's student culture, this extended to sportswear becoming a powerful symbol of status as well.

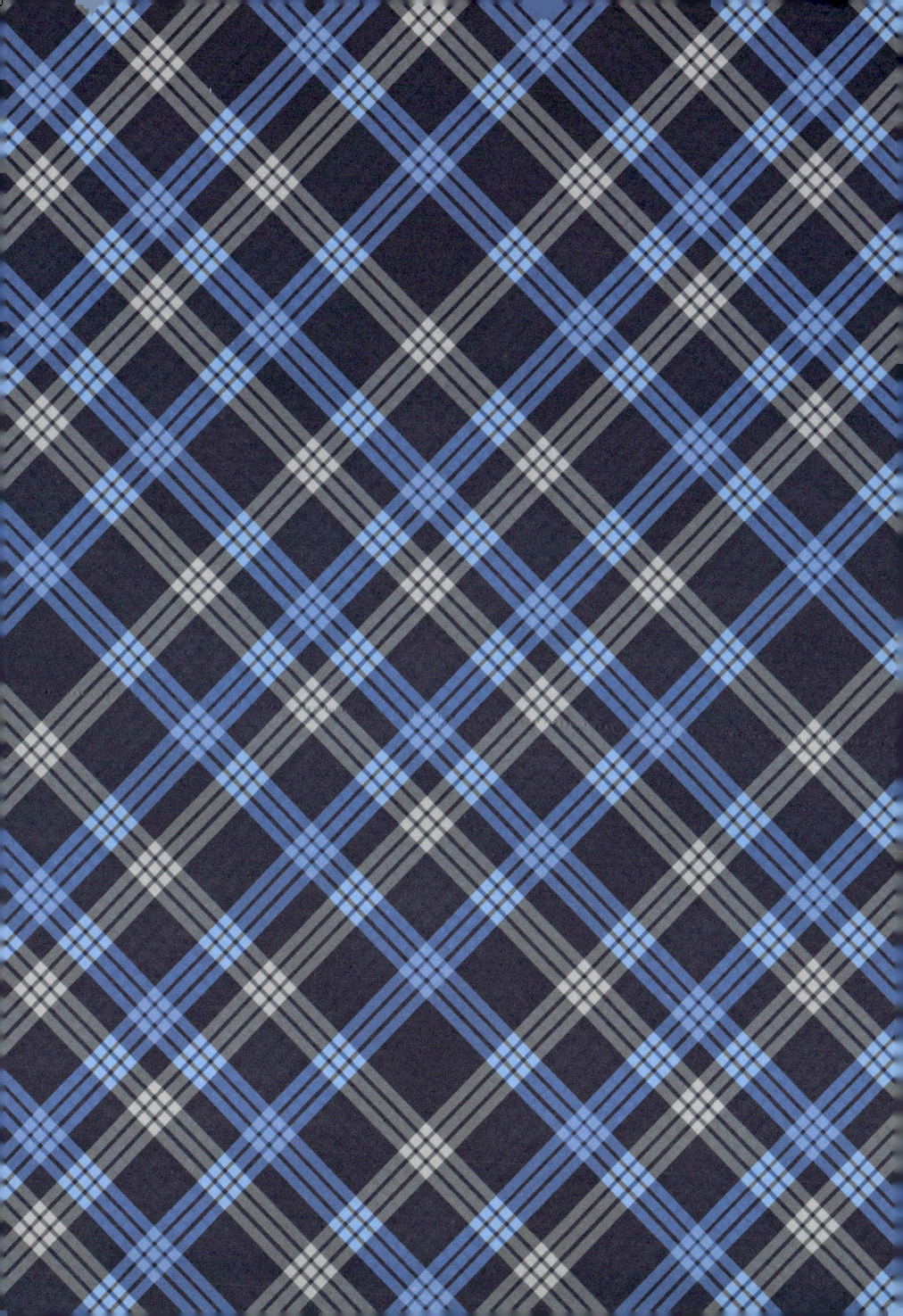

Company versus Customer

Brooks Brothers was a true disruptor in the fashion world, pioneering preppy style by providing the raw ingredients to the Ivy League look. Yet, as is a common thread through preppy style's evolution, it was as much about styling as it was about the pieces. While the essentials of preppy style remained relatively unchanged and evolved slowly, how those pieces were put together constantly shifted. This was due to culture on college campuses, predominantly at Princeton. In the early years, Brooks Brothers set the standard for what to wear, while young men—vying for status and conformity in their Waspy East Coast environments—showed how these pieces could be worn in new and entirely modern ways.

Here were style-setting students who had the money and means for both quality and quantity. Advertisements for Brooks Brothers and Franks Brothers—a luxury shoe company—filled yearbooks, newspapers, and athletic programs. Spending big on preppy pieces was something Princeton men were supremely good at. Better still, was having their coveted seal of approval. Brands and magazines used the university's name to sell everything from shoes to shirt collars. Take E.E. Taylor Corporation's "Princetonian" shoe: being advertised as coming "from the campus of the country's collegiate fashion center" appealed to students at rival schools, and aided in making it one of the brand's best-selling designs of 1934. In *Life* magazine's 1938 article titled "Princeton Boys Dress in Uniform," they explained how "tailors and haberdashers watch Princeton students closely [and] admit they are style leaders." After all, many men only embraced a new piece once they saw other men wearing it.

As it turned out, if you wanted preppy inspiration, you were best to look at the Princeton crowd. With an ample bank account and the need to dress the part, it's no surprise they were owners of a well-honed wardrobe. Whether your preppy lineup consists of a sport coat, argyle sweater, or anything in-between, it's likely they were popularized at Princeton first.

2

The Evolution of Prep

"Preppies don't have to be rich, Caucasian, frequenters of Bermuda, or ace tennis players," states the initiation at the beginning of *The Official Preppy Handbook.*

How did a style once so synonymous with the affluent, white students attending leafy Ivy League campuses end up becoming a worldwide phenomenon embraced by so many? A look back through the aesthetic's illustrious history shows the evolution from its prestigious American college origins to the streets of Tokyo and its influence on the Civil Rights Movement, before reemerging on fashion runways throughout the decades. The key to the success of preppy style has been to recognize its roots, delve into its past, and pay homage to tradition, but to constantly reinvent certain aspects.

J. Press and "The Yale Man"

There was a wave building, a preppy movement, led by brands and styled by college students. Along with Brooks Brothers, J. Press was one of two classic American clothing brands that helped shape the subculture in the early years. Founded in 1902 by Latvian immigrant Jacobi Press, he opened up shop on Yale University's New Haven campus in Connecticut. Setting the standard for preppy attire since the beginning, J. Press was (and still is) renowned for its "Shaggy Dog" Shetland wool sweaters, repp ties, Oxford button-down shirts, well-cut navy blazers with brass buttons, and tweed sport coats adorned with vertical stripes.

Despite both brands being preppy, there were differences between the two. Brooks Brothers's selection of clothing was much broader than its smaller rival, offering the essential components of the Ivy League look and much more. J. Press, on the other hand, was strictly Ivy, and therefore argued by some as being a purer purveyor of the style. As well as being larger, Brooks Brothers catered more toward urban culture than the country-focused J. Press. Lastly, Brooks Brothers may have been favored by affluent Princetonians, but it was J. Press's ability to adapt to the more restricted—yet still wealthy—allowances of other campuses with its less expensive pieces that helped proliferate the aesthetic further.

Trendsetters at Princeton were decked out in the sack suits of New York–based Brooks Brothers, but undergraduates were doing preppy their own way in New Haven. They developed a close relationship

with the clothing stores near campus on Elm and York Streets, namely J. Press and Fenn-Feinstein. Students not only wanted clothing stores to get them preppy pieces that were trending but also give them access to new styles they hadn't seen before. In turn, stores needed to keep a watchful eye on what was being worn on campus to know what was popular. Straight-hanging coats with natural shoulders was one style in particular that came to define the Yale look. Men at Yale (there were no Yale women until the fall of 1969) accompanied it with pieces that were much sportier and more casual than Brooks Brothers's designs, like J. Press's snap-brim hats combined with horn-rimmed glasses.

In the decades that followed, *Life* magazine cited New Haven as the home of the Ivy League look, writing, "Sometimes regarded as more of a club than a clothes shop, J. Press is delighted rather than dismayed that its look is now capturing the country." Soon, even Macy's wanted a piece of the action; the department store giant started selling clothing on York Street, opposite Yale's Sterling Memorial Library. In an effort to convince the Yale community to shop, Macy's confidently stated in a 1941 ad that it can "bring you the widest possible assortments of clothes that are high in prestige, low in price." By the 1950s and '60s, it was simple to spot where a Yale man shopped just by his shirt: a plain pocket signaled Fenn-Feinstein, while a pocket with a flap meant J. Press. If the shirt had no pocket at all, then it was Brooks Brothers.

G.I. Bill and the Golden Era

In the years following the Second World War, college campuses were flooded with a new wave of students—and with it came a new preppy classic. The Servicemen's Readjustment Act of 1944 (also known as the G.I. Bill) provided a range of benefits for those returning from service, including financial support for higher education, unemployment insurance, and housing. About 2.2 million veterans, many from blue-collar backgrounds who previously wouldn't have been able to afford to go, enrolled into college, and they needed to dress the part. Brooks Brothers and J. Press became the first port of call. Versatile basics such as Oxford shirts and cable-knit sweaters were exactly what they needed to blend in with a society that saw itself as being socially privileged.

It wasn't just former American soldiers adopting the look of the Ivy League elite. Tired of strict army uniforms, veterans brought with them a more informal approach to dressing. Many attended classes in their government-issue tan cotton khaki pants, and the rugged, utilitarian design caught the eye of the fashion-conscious Ivy League set. They were also referred to as chinos, which takes its name from a cotton-twill fabric originally from China and also used for military uniforms there. Whether they called them chinos or khakis, preps realized that they were versatile enough to wear to the lecture hall or play Frisbee in on the quad at lunch.

There were plenty of khakis available across the country to meet demand. Army surplus stores were full of them, which made it easy for those who hadn't served to get their hands on a pair. Dressier than

What Is Khaki?

Unbeknownst to some, khaki is a color, not a fabric. It's often used interchangeably for the word "chinos," but is in fact not a garment of clothing. The term itself is from the Persian word *khâk* which means "soil," and also from a term in Hindustani that means "soil-colored." Starting as military uniforms and evolving into statement chinos, the color is now used to make shirts, jackets, and even socks.

denim, but less formal than suit pants, khakis became a fixture with the young students at Princeton who began pairing them with loafers, shirts, and blazers (just picture Ben Affleck, Matt Damon, Brendan Fraser, and others in the 1992 film *School Ties*). The trend was picked up by the rest of the Ivy League schools, onto historically Black universities, and—alongside the rest of the Ivy League look—into mainstream culture. As the aesthetic entered its Golden Era of the 1950s and '60s, khakis (along with the T-shirt, another G.I. favorite) paved the way for a much more casual approach to prep.

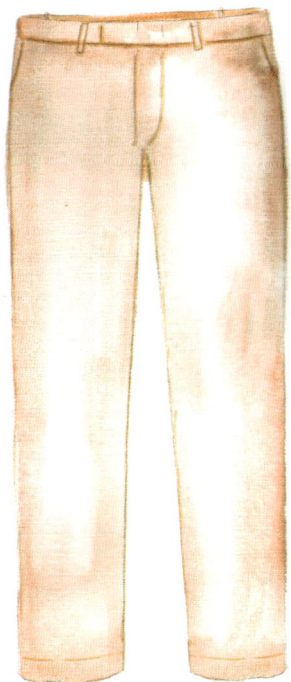

The Vassar Girl

The Seven Sisters colleges—Barnard, Bryn Mawr, Mount Holyoke, Smith, Radcliffe, Vassar, and Wellesley—were a prestigious group of American colleges that was founded to be the female equivalent of the then all-male Ivy League schools. For a long time, preppy style served men more than women. That is until the Ivy League look heavily influenced the female students who attended the Seven Sisters colleges, but they had to borrow from the boys if they wanted to be part of it.

In the 1930s, women attending the Seven Sisters colleges began challenging traditional expectations of dress codes. They adopted elements of the preppy look as a means to show intellect and that they too were part of the elite. Just as Princeton was known for setting menswear trends, it was Vassar that established itself as the fashion leader for women. Founded in 1861 in Poughkeepsie, New York, Vassar College was established "to be to women what Harvard and Yale are to young men." In 1937, *Life* magazine posted an article centered around what the girls at Vassar were wearing: men's Brooks Brothers sweaters, tweed skirts, polo coats, and tennis shoes.

While Vassar didn't become fully coeducational until 1969, a small number of young men were admitted before that on the G.I. Bill. Similar to the effect the "Vassar Vets" had at the male-dominated Ivy League colleges, their relaxed clothing choices of khaki pants, jeans, and Bermuda shorts had a notable impact on the way prep was interpreted by Vassar women. The fathers, brothers, and even boyfriends of Seven Sisters students were often Ivy educated and helped to disseminate this preppy style further. For years, women had watched as men built their collegiate wardrobe around Brooks Brothers, J. Press, and Fenn-Feinstein,

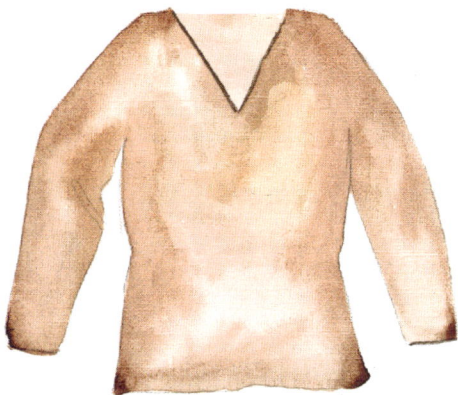

and now they relied on the same stores for their very own pieces. With the rise in popularity of classic menswear pieces on the Seven Sisters campuses, brands and retailers began catering to the growing demand. In 1949, Brooks Brothers acknowledged the large number of women who wanted to wear the brand and debuted a pink Oxford that was cut to fit the female form.

By the 1950s, the "Vassar Girl" in popular culture became a phenomenon. During this decade, the media cultivated a cultural and sartorial icon, but there was little visual representation of preppy style seen around campus. Take Marilyn Monroe in the 1959 comedy *Some Like It Hot*, which saw the actress pretending to be a wealthy Vassar student. Hiding her working-class background to impress Tony Curtis's character, who in turn pretends to be a millionaire, Marilyn Monroe imitates the stereotypical rich, white, smart, and attractive debutante with high heels and elegant gowns.

In reality, Vassar girls had created their own unofficial campus uniform, and it was almost identical to men's Ivy League style. Bermuda shorts were paired with a Brooks Brothers Oxford shirt, a classic Vassar blazer, knee socks, and loafers—although the college did demand skirts were still worn for dinner and any event or trip off campus. It was this distinctive look of real Vassar students that was captured in 1957 when they were photographed as models for the annual *Vogue* college issue.

On and Off Campus

The book *Seven Sisters Style: The All-American Preppy Look* by Rebecca C. Tuite was released in 2014. Within it lay evidence of what was unseen, or intentionally not photographed, of the fashion during day-to-day life at a Seven Sisters campus. While the Vassar Girl changed the stagnant uniforms of collegiate women to adopt the look and sophistication of Ivy League men, Tuite found something unexpected during her time at Vassar College in 2006. "Of course I showed up in my best Jackie Kennedy-esque outfit, and realized people wore pj's to class." She goes on to describe the three types of iconic Seven Sisters looks: the tomboy, the prepster, and the ladylike-society girl.

In public, Vassar Girls came out in their best Brooks Brothers pieces, sometimes taken directly from the closets of their brothers, fathers, or boyfriends. But in the privacy of the campus, intelligence reined supreme and fashion took second place.

Lilly Pulitzer,
"The Queen of Prep"

By the late 1950s, preppy style had expanded outside of Ivy League and the Seven Sisters colleges. Its popularity rose in areas where students already enjoyed vacations at their families' estates, such as Palm Beach. The aesthetic had been slowly growing in the glamorous Florida town for decades—to no one's surprise, Brooks Brothers had opened its third location here (after New York City and Newport, Rhode Island) back in 1924, where the Everglades Club had been attracting socialites, celebrities, and royalty to its tennis and golf tournaments, parties, galas, and balls for years.

It was in this iconic beach town, among the sunny weather, ocean-view mansions, glossy green lawns, and swaying palm trees, that the classic preppy look was reinvented once more. The bright colors that were so prevalent here inspired the Ivy Leaguers, and in turn the brands that outfitted them. In fact, it all began with one fashion designer in particular: Lilly Pulitzer.

The Dress That Started It All

In 1959, at a stand in Palm Beach, socialite Lilly Pulitzer started selling juice from oranges sourced from her husband's citrus groves. Finding her clothes continually ruined by fruit stains, she realized she needed dresses in fabrics that were so bold and colorful, the juice splashes would be harder to notice. Her dressmaker turned her idea into reality, and she started to wear the brightly printed "Lilly" shift dress to work. Her immensely cheerful designs were a hit with wealthy customers who, instead of wearing the high-end couture they had access to, requested their own dresses in the boldest colors imaginable. The short, sleeveless dresses were unlike anything else on the market and ignited a Palm Beach fashion craze. "It was a total change of life for me," Pulitzer told *W* Magazine in 2008. "I entered it with no business sense . . . It was just something that I all of a sudden took over."

The "Queen of Prep," as she became known, utilized her status (her family came from the Standard Oil fortune and her husband was part of the Pulitzer publishing family) and network of society women to situate her brand among the elite, both in Palm Beach and New York. The Lilly Pulitzer brand reached new heights when her former classmate and First Lady at the time, Jackie Kennedy, was photographed wearing one of her polka-dot dresses as she vacationed in Capri. The brand was boosted even further when Jackie Kennedy graced the cover of *Life* magazine wearing a gingham version in 1962. A year later, the popularity of her clothes meant Lilly had warranted a *Life* spread of her own.

Bright and Bold Prints

Lilly partnered with a screen-printing shop called Key West Hand Prints, which would become instrumental in establishing the brand's vibrant aesthetic. This is where the other big name in the story of Lilly Pulitzer and her carefree preppy resort wear comes in: designer Suzie Zuzek, the textile genius (and formally trained artist) behind the eclectic, playful prints. It's said that in 1962, while working as head designer for the shop, Zuzek was approached by a barefoot Lilly Pulitzer (she rarely wore shoes) who ordered three hundred yards (274 m) of a Zuzek print on the spot. But then as soon as she returned home to Palm Beach, Lilly called and immediately changed the order to three thousand yards (2,743 m). The pair worked together for the next twenty-five years, creating preppy clothing in bold patterns that became the hallmark of the brand. In a 1971 interview in *The Palm Beach Post*, Pulitzer said, "We were a real shock to everyone. People thought the Lilly dress was a fad that would last about two years . . . We just picked up steam and kept going." According to *The New York Times*, at its height in the 1960s and '70s, the brand had sales of more than $15 million.

After decades of women corseting themselves to fit the clothes, Lilly's shifts loosened it all up. Fashion reflected the profound social changes that were happening in the late 1950s and '60s: the Civil Rights Movement, the anti-war movement, and the second wave of feminism—the latter which inspired women to step outside of more traditional roles. Lilly Pulitzer was one such woman, who, by tapping into her entrepreneurial spirit, not only revolutionized the fashion world with her signature bold, joyful prints but also helped shape and brighten preppy style along the way.

Black Ivy

Prep's peak came at a time when many were challenging the status quo. The Second World War had accelerated social change in America, and Black servicemen's fight against fascism in Nazi Germany had brought America's own ideals of democracy and racial equality into focus. Additionally, Black migration from the South to the North, where the right to vote was available, exposed the racial divisions and disparities among the states.

It may be a style deeply rooted in exclusive Waspy establishments, but prep is the foundational American style which Black people have long been a part of: Preppy played a major role in pro–Civil Rights activism in the mid-1950s and '60s. The quiet, conservative uniform of the college-educated elite was used by young Black people as a way of challenging outdated perceptions—and prejudices—of their place in society. Over the years, the look within this culture became known as Black Ivy, and its importance in shaping preppy style has been almost forgotten.

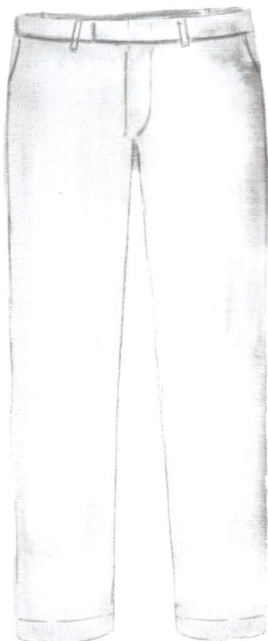

Ivy at Historically Black Universities and Colleges

Dressing in preppy style wasn't new to Black society, and it didn't begin with the Civil Rights Movement. In fact, it started exactly where traditional Ivy did: on campus. Students who attended historically Black Universities and Colleges (HBCUs) like Morehouse, Howard, and Spelman—a women's college—embodied a preppy style all their own. Although they followed similar style codes to those attending WASP colleges, Black students changed and enhanced them. Students continued to wear the Ivy style after they graduated from HBCUs, transitioning the look into the everyday as they moved on to careers like politics and law.

Attending college was almost necessary to be exposed to Black Ivy, though it was also picked up from country clubs. Segregation meant that Black people weren't allowed to join these typically exclusionary clubs, but were often employed there. This merging of cultures led to a further evolution and expansion of the style. What's often left from the wider narrative around preppy style is that Black professionals like Harvard-educated Dr. W. E. B. Du Bois had been wearing elements of the Ivy League look as early as the interwar years. Its growing popularity in mainstream culture meant that Hollywood actors like Sidney Poitier and athletes like tennis champion Arthur Ashe were sporting it too.

One particular champion of the Black Ivy look was jazz music legend Miles Davis, who originally wore it with the aim of presenting himself as a serious artist. With his slim-cut, flat-front pants, soft-shouldered jackets, button-down shirts, and Bass Weejun loafers, he was the epitome of Black Ivy cool. Becoming a key influencer for Black preps, it became less about students at Morehouse College wanting to look like they went to Princeton and more about wanting to look like Miles Davis.

Fashioning the Protest

The traditional preppy look evolved with the emergence of the Civil Rights Movement. Whether intentionally or unintentionally, those involved in the movement dressed in preppy clothing to demonstrate the equality and respect that was being denied to them in other ways. Dressing in a style that had its roots in the affluent and educated of white society drew attention to the cause and challenged the racist preconceptions of mainstream America, a strategy often referred to as respectability politics.

The aesthetics adopted by certain groups within the Civil Rights Movement created a powerful cognitive dissonance for supporters of Jim Crow, disrupting their deeply held belief that Black people were meant to present (and dress) themselves as inferior. In the early 1950s, many activists used this subversive force of style as their weapon of choice. Dr. Martin Luther King Jr. was one of them.

Throughout his career as a leader of the movement, Dr. Martin Luther King Jr. visited all the Ivy League schools—Yale, Princeton, Harvard, Columbia, Cornell, UPenn, Dartmouth, and Brown—advocating against poverty, racism, and militarism. Alongside other leaders like James Forman and Ralph Abernathy, he was frequently seen wearing neat suits, straight ties, trench coats, and capped brogues—matching the dress codes set by white leaders in government, many of whom were Ivy League alumni. Preppy style became prevalent at marches, boycotts, and staged sit-ins at lunch counters, with young Black men and women tailoring it to fit the movement's needs.

Dressing to Fit the Mold

By the 1960s, Black students from the Student Nonviolent Coordinating Committee (SNCC) began traveling from northern states to the South in an effort to increase voter registration in rural areas. As college-educated activists marched shoulder to shoulder with working class and rural Black Americans, they shed their flannel suits and dresses in exchange for utility pieces that the sharecroppers in the South were wearing. Donning the same chambray shirts, jeans, and overalls suddenly became a point of solidarity. The look said that even farm workers in the remotest rural South should have the same rights as anyone else in the United States. As a result, workwear became an essential part of the Black Ivy look and, in turn, worked its way into preppy style as a whole.

While many emulated the style of Ivy Leaguers in order to fight for their rights, others chose to visually represent the movement in a different way. Members of the Black Panther Party refused to conform to the respectability roots of the early phase, and instead, chose the Dashiki (a traditional African shirt), turtleneck sweater, black leather jacket, and an afro tucked into a beret over repp ties and Oxford shirts. After the assassinations of Malcolm X in 1965 and Martin Luther King Jr. in 1968, the realization was that no amount of adhering to white dress codes would diminish racism. The uniform of the Black Panther Party, complete with a symbolic fist in the air, replaced Black Ivy style as the look that defined the movement.

More Than a Fashion Statement

The Black Ivy era of preppy's evolution showed how style can be an intrinsic part of a radical, political, and social movement. It proved that fashion is more than just clothing, and how we dress can be loaded with significance, power, and meaning. Black culture took Ivy clothing away from its elitist confines, remixing and reenvisioning it into something distinctive and instantly recognizable in its own right; yet still connected to prep.

Although the Black community's influence on shaping the preppy look has been relatively undocumented, many in the fashion industry are beginning to acknowledge and appreciate how it informs the style we know—and wear—today. British brand Drake's capsule collection with Jason Jules, author of 2022 *Black Ivy: A Revolt in Style*, highlighted that there are elements and ideas of Black Ivy that are truly timeless. In the same year, Ralph Lauren celebrated the style legacy of two historically Black colleges: Morehouse and Spelman. Inspired by the schools' rich heritage and esteemed traditions, Ralph Lauren's limited-edition collection (complete with an all-Black campaign cast) was the first of its kind. Explaining the collaboration, Ralph Lauren said, "It's about sharing a more complete and authentic portrait of American style and of the American—ensuring stories of Black life and experiences are embedded in the inspiration and aspiration of our brand."

The Myth of
Take Ivy

By this point, preppy had long left the confines of campus and had been slowly making its mark on American culture in many different ways for decades. Alongside Black Ivy, other changes were being made to the look. Plaid was becoming more popular and rugby shirts had joined the lineup of sporty separates that were now being worn away from the field. Preppy had also given rise to an offshoot, Americana, which soon became synonymous with denim jeans and bowling shirts. But prep was soon to acquire a new global status thanks to a 1965 book called *Take Ivy*.

Who Brought Ivy Style to Japan?

How—and why—did Shosuke Ishizu manage to have such an influence on this era of prep's evolution? It all starts, surprisingly, in the Chinese port city of Tianjin. Ishizu moved there from Okayama, Japan, for a job running a successful fashion store called Ogawa Yoko. However, when the war took a turning point against Japan in 1943, the store's Japanese employees closed it to enlist. Ishizu left with them, working in a munitions factory in China. In 1945, Ishizu became friends with an American soldier named O'Brien who spoke of his life at Princeton University—this was to be Ishizu's first initiation to Ivy League style.

Fast-forward to postwar Japan, 1946, when Ishizu returned to discover his hometown of Okayama completely destroyed. A fresh start was the only option. Utilizing the experiences he acquired from selling clothing back in Tianjin, Ishizu started working at Renown—Japan's largest undergarment producer—before earning a position as a menswear designer in its Osaka showroom. After creating the first replicas of American-style pieces (blue jeans and pocket T-shirts), Ishizu left Renown to start his own premium menswear brand called Ishizu Shoten. At the time Ishizu opened his first store, the Korean War started to revive Japan's economy.

Shosuke's Preppy Upbringing

Shosuke Ishizu's father, Kensuke, was born into a prominent family and had an obsession with Western clothing. He went to university in Tokyo, wore expensive British-style bespoke suits, and spent his nights at the dance halls. Fast-forward to when Shosuke moved away from his family to go to Tianjin, the store he worked at sold Western gentlemen clothing. So we might have his father to thank for instilling in him an interest in preppy fashion.

The VAN Jacket

Ishizu Shoten's high-end sports coats soon became popular with wealthy families from the Ashiya suburb. Yet in an era of made-to-measure suiting, the brand's off-the-rack pieces suffered from a lack of interest outside of this affluent clientele. In 1951, Ishizu knew that he needed to rebrand and, remembering Ivy League, he called it "VAN Jacket."

In 1959, VAN took inspiration from Brooks Brothers's No. 1 Sack Suit to produce its "Ivy Model" design. It was the complete opposite of Japanese fashion at the time. Popular jazz musicians were mainly in one-button suit jackets with oversized shoulders, while Japanese students were dressed in a traditional black jacket and pant uniform: the gakuran. Although the more progressive department stores were quick to stock VAN, being the first brand to recreate Ivy League clothing in Japan came with its challenges. Ishizu needed to overcome the sentimentality of Japanese men in the early 1950s, who weren't keen to go against the grain when it came to clothes—even if they were still just suits. Realizing that his generation would always prefer tailor-made clothing over off-the-rack designs, Ishizu turned his attention to the younger generation who were relatively uncatered to when it came to fashion.

Ishizu realized that magazines devoted to men's fashion were worthwhile promotional tools for brands. He joined the editorial team of Japan's first men's fashion magazine, *Otoko no Fukushoku*, in 1954 and used it as a platform to push Ivy League style to Japan's large youth population. He also used it to sell brands closely tied to the publication, with advertisements for VAN weaved in and out of the entire magazine. Later renamed *Men's Club* to appeal to the youth's fascination with Western culture, the publication's shift in focus taught men why and how to dress better and supported the style in reaching mass-market territory.

VAN released a full collection of prep-inspired pieces in 1962 that were designed to be coordinated together—Oxford button-downs, tweed jackets, navy blazers, and striped university scarves. Creating different items under a single brand was another pioneering move, as the industry had previously been divided into brands that exclusively made single pieces such as ties or shirts. In 1963, Toshiyuki Kurosu began a column in *Men's Club* called "Ivy Leaguers on the Street." As Japan's foremost Ivy expert and a keen follower of Ishizu, Kurosu and a photographer were among the first to document those on the streets of Ginza who dressed like East Coast preps.

Heibon Punch, the Miyuki Tribe, and the Tokyo Olympics

After being covered so extensively in *Men's Club*, by 1964, Ivy League was a burgeoning trend. It was when new youth culture magazine *Heibon Punch* launched in the same year that proved to be a turning point for the style. Each weekly edition was highly anticipated by university students, and it attracted a larger following than *Men's Club*, with the debut issue selling 620,000 copies, and a circulation of one million within two years. To support the growing interest in Ivy, Ishizu was brought in to write articles about menswear.

The instant success of *Heibon Punch* meant that it was the fashion that Japanese middle-class teenagers wanted to be seen in. They headed to the most renowned retailer for Ivy clothing: VAN. The brand's flagship store was based in the Ginza neighborhood of Tokyo, where groups of young people wearing the ubiquitous button-down shirts, chinos, and penny loafers would park themselves on Miyuki Street. The brand's famous rolled-up paper shopping bag with the iconic VAN logo even became a sought-after accessory. So much so, some who were unable to afford it simply put VAN stickers on old rice bags to be part of the growing trend. The press nicknamed them the Miyuki Tribe (also known as Miyuki-zoku), with the postwar usage of *zoku* as a connotation of a delinquent subculture.

As the number of teens in the Miyuki Tribe increased, so did the public furor. It was the year Tokyo was hosting the Olympics, and the Miyuki Tribe was portrayed in the press as being a national embarrassment. Parents attempted to ban Ivy style from schools, and requests were made to prohibit VAN retailers from selling to students. Yet this only served to make Ivy more attractive to the Japanese teen masses. After years of trying, Ishizu's efforts had paid off. VAN went on to become Japan's leading brand in the 1960s, and Ivy style was finally cool.

The popularity with teenagers caused a barrier that Ishizu had to overcome. He was concerned that the Ivy style he was trying to sell to the mainstream would always be negatively associated with the Miyuki Tribe. He hoped to change public opinion with the uniforms of Japanese athletes and ground staff at the 1964 Summer Olympics opening ceremony. They paraded into the stadium led by their country's flag and dressed in three-two roll blazers—a type of jacket that features three buttonholes and three buttons but with only two buttons meant to be used—offset with striped ties, hats, and white pants and skirts with matching red piping. It was a radical look for the time. The brightness of the red blazers shocked many as, up until this point, Japanese men had never worn the color. However, the way it evoked Japan's national flag imparted a sense of pride, and the occasion marked the beginning of a new movement in fashion.

VAN was one of the few brands selling these three-button jackets, which department stores soon requested to stock. Although the Olympics had helped, Ishizu still needed to remove any misconceptions

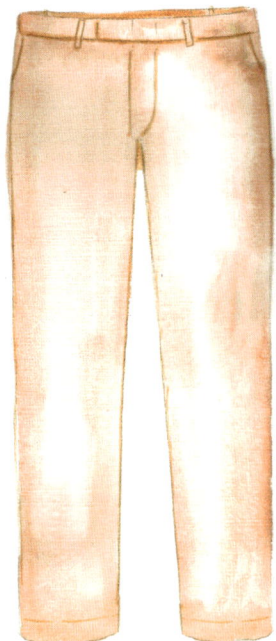

around Ivy caused by the Miyuki Tribe in order to sell the concept. While discussing ways to improve the image of Ivy League clothing, an idea to make a film was born. The film would show that actual Ivy League students were much better dressed than the teenagers in Ginza. An ideal way to distill, package, and sell preppy clothing—first to Japan, then to the rest of the world.

Take Ivy

In May 1965, Ishizu gathered together two editors, Toshiyuki Kurosu and Hajime Hasegawa, and a photographer Teruyoshi Hayashida. The four-man team left for the United States with the goal of filming the natural style of Ivy League students. They had planned to go to all eight of the university campuses on the East Coast, yet time constraints meant they were only able to visit six. This wasn't the only problem the team faced. Time had moved on, and the original Ivy style was now long gone. The tailored formality so eagerly adopted in Japan was nowhere to be seen. It had largely been replaced with something much more casual: untucked shirts, shorts with shoes, and no socks. Comfort was first and foremost, and it just so happens it had an effortless, timeless look. In Japan, Ivy was very much about the rules, compared to America where it was a nearly unconscious style.

Despite the shift in expectations, Ishizu still needed to pursue a notion of America that no longer existed. The team returned to Japan to work out how the footage they captured of dressed-down American students could be used to promote the virtues of Ivy League style. As work began on editing the film, the idea of turning Hayashida's photos into a book was born. The resulting style manual, *Take Ivy*, was carefully manufactured to match the particular vision needed to win over the

Japanese public, as well as stockists, distributors, and retailers. The photos in *Take Ivy* show the students as being dressed much less formal than those who had come before. It's this lack of formality that became the first step in preppy style gradually becoming more relaxed. Despite Ivy League students being more casually dressed than expected, *Take Ivy* conveyed that this nonchalant approach to preppy dressing actually signaled status.

The book was a collection of candid photographs that documented a golden era of Ivy League campus life. Whether strolling across the quad, relaxing at the boathouse, or grabbing lunch in the cafeteria, *Take Ivy* showed students distinctively dressed in the pinnacle of preppy style—varsity jackets, penny loafers, madras Bermuda shorts, chinos, and Oxford button-down shirts. The book's aim was summed up in a caption under a photograph of students: "Together they represent what we hoped to find on our fact-finding trip: the epitome of daily dress for Ivy Leaguers."

Take Ivy ended up being a huge success. After struggling for over a decade to bring America's preppy aesthetic to the Japanese people, Ishizu finally changed public opinion. In the years that followed, *Take Ivy* triggered the start of men's style in Japan. It became a source of inspiration for many *Men's Club* articles and read by those who relied on magazines to guide them on the right way to wear preppy clothing. By the '80s, the Japanese evolved past simply copying American style and developed their own take on preppy style, called *Ametora*—a Japanese slang word combining "American" and "traditional." Ametora was a genre of clothing that incorporated not only Ivy League–inspired Brooks Brothers suiting, but Japanification versions of any American clothing tradition, including jeans, rock 'n' roll, and West Coast outdoor gear. The Japanese improved on the quality, pushed fabric technology, and used innovative production techniques to reinterpret the different styles of clothing—making them their own.

Copies of *Take Ivy* became highly sought-after, and when a small-run reprint came out in Japan in 2006, it sold out almost immediately. Forty-five years after it was first published in Japan, it was then released by Brooklyn publisher powerHouse in an English-language edition for the first time in 2010. Described by *The New York Times* as "a treasure of fashion insiders," this even more influential translated version sold over fifty thousand copies worldwide and turned the book into a viral phenomenon. It was proudly displayed on the shelves of Ralph Lauren and J.Crew stores and sparked a new wave of interest in preppy style.

The Godfather of Japanese Prep

Often deemed the godfather of the Ivy League fashion movement, Ishizu played a key role in bringing preppy style to Japan. From *Men's Club* to *Take Ivy*, he was involved in every project related to Ivy League fashion and helped convince the masses that it was a legitimate aesthetic to buy into. By laying the framework for preppy style, Ishizu set the pattern for how Japan would import, consume, and modify American fashion for years to come. Eventually, the Japanese would make preppy style their own, elevating it through manufacturing practices that set a new quality standard.

Over time, preppy style seeped into the basics of Japanese fashion culture. However, this meant that VAN, once the standard-bearer for the Japanese Ivy look, was not the only one making it. More companies imitated the button-down shirt, sweaters, navy jackets, and flat-front chinos that were so synonymous with VAN in the 1960s, and its brand power started to decline. VAN declared bankruptcy in 1978. And in 2005, Shosuke Ishizu died at the age of ninety-three. By then, millions of Japanese men were wearing Ivy League pieces as their basic style, and its influence over renowned Japanese fashion labels is still evident today as seen in brands such as BEAMS and Uniqlo.

3

Prep Icons

The influence Black Ivy and Shosuke Ishizu had on the evolution of preppy style often gets overlooked, but there's one person who never does: Ralph Lauren.

He may not be the sole inventor of the quintessentially American, preppy look, but images of his enduring brand are likely what spring to mind first when you think of it. Ralph Lauren—still going strong after more than fifty years—is responsible for packaging up prep to the masses and cultivating it into an international uniform that endures today.

Ralph on the Rise

Ralph Lifshitz, as he was then known, was born in the Bronx to Jewish immigrants from Belarus. Raised in the Norwood neighborhood in the 1940s and '50s, in a four-room apartment overlooking Mosholu Parkway with his three siblings, he was just a few blocks away from another future designer stalwart, Calvin Klein. Even as a teenager, he had a fascination with fashion, often scouring secondhand shops for clothes that helped him emulate the preppy look of New York's upper-class students. "I was always inspired by those kind of prep-school people and their clothes," Lauren once said. "By classic things, by the way those people looked and dressed. Maybe because I didn't have it, I always reached for it."

When he was sixteen, he and his brother Jerry legally changed their last name to Lauren. It wasn't pretentious or a bid to become a WASP; instead, it was down to being constantly teased at school over their unfortunate-sounding surname. "My given name has the word s--t in it. When I was a kid, the other kids would make a lot of fun of me. It was a tough name. That's why I decided to change it," Lauren told Oprah Winfrey in 2002 for an issue of *O, The Oprah Magazine*. "Then people said, 'Did you change your name because you don't want to be Jewish?' I said, 'Absolutely not. That's not what it's about.'" Yet changing his name was something Lauren often regretted, believing it had made people question his integrity over the years. The designer once famously said, "Because I believe in authenticity, it seems inauthentic to have changed your name."

In the same interview, he spoke on his fashion taste and what others thought about his interest in the Ivy League look. He was criticized and said, "There were also people who thought that because I was Jewish, I had no right to create these preppy clothes. Harvard, Yale, Princeton: 'Why do you like these kind of things?'" people would ask him.

After attending nearby DeWitt Clinton High School (where he wrote "millionaire" as one of his life goals in the yearbook), he studied business at the downtown Baruch campus of City College before completing a brief stint in the army. When he was twenty-four, and despite having no fashion experience, Lauren took a sales job at Brooks Brothers on Madison Avenue. It proved to be the catalyst for Lauren's journey into redefining preppy style. "Brooks Brothers was the foundation, and I revived it," Lauren said in a 1985 interview with *New York* magazine. Years before he started his own brand, the visionary designer was already garnering attention for his bold, Ivy League–inspired fashion, and as the *Daily News-Record* put it, his "taste seems to be a season's jump ahead of the market." The newspaper published a profile of Lauren as a young, trendsetting salesman in its column "The Professional Touch" in 1964. It noted how Lauren wore "riding pants of heavy but supple corduroy with suede patches" and a "double-breasted navy blazer with straight, rather than peaked lapel."

While working at Brooks Brothers, which Lauren described as being "like an Ivy League School," he realized that everyone around him was wearing button-down shirts and narrow ties. Going against what was trending at the time, Lauren wanted spread collars, wide ties, and shaped suits; but they were nowhere to be found. So, he decided to make them himself.

Making History

At twenty-six, Lauren started his own line. In a nod to the affluence associated with one of the most elite sports in the world, when naming his brand he landed on the polished and sophisticated "Polo." Lauren was famously never formally trained and couldn't sew, stitch, or sketch, but he had an eye. In his early business, he focused on creating unusually wide, European-style ties out of a one-room office in the Empire State Building. They were innovative four-inch-wide (10 cm) designs that were made from high-end, unexpected fabrics, and patterns such as classic repp stripes and rich prints. The repp tie, with its diagonal stripes, was already a cornerstone of every prep wardrobe. Lauren reflected on the start of his career for *RL Mag*, stating: "At the time—this was 1967—I felt there was no tie like the ones I wanted to do. My tie was wide at a time when men wore narrow ties, like today. I searched for unusual fabrics, so they were unique. Men loved them. They bounced off the racks."

Lauren sold his ties to some of the most prestigious names in men's clothing, including Paul Stuart, Neiman Marcus, and Bloomingdale's, hand delivering the orders to the stores dressed in an old bomber jacket and jeans. During that first year, the stores loved the ties so much that after selling $500,000 worth of them, they still wanted more.

Moving on to preppy essentials like shirts, suits, and sport coats with lapels, Lauren matched them to the width of the ties. The line was so successful that in 1970, the Polo by Ralph Lauren shop opened within Bloomingdale's. It was the department store's first ever boutique dedicated to one designer, and Lauren was involved in every detail, right down to the Ivy League–inspired wood-paneled walls.

By 1971, less than five years after the launch of his first tie collection, Ralph Lauren expanded his brand and opened a Polo boutique on Beverly Hills' storied Rodeo Drive. It made him the first American designer to have a freestanding store.

A Vision of Americana

Ralph Lauren continued his airtight vision of Americana with the launch of a small women's collection in 1971 (with the full collection to come a year later) which took cues from menswear with smart tailored shirts and the now-iconic Polo logo debuting on the cuff. "When I started to make menswear, women were always asking, 'Can you make that for me?'" Ralph Lauren said. "I think I heard their voices . . ." From changing existing styles to inventing something new altogether, Lauren was making huge contributions to the ever-changing preppy aesthetic. At the same time, the designer's own Polo look became more distinctive and defined, focusing on an enduring appreciation of all things that have timeless style. Ralph Lauren was beginning to move and change fashion in a simple way; and it all started with the wide tie.

An Icon of American Style

As Ralph Lauren's vision for American style spread across the country and the world, it couldn't have been more prep. In fact, in 1972, Ralph Lauren took inspiration from the athletes at Ivy League campuses to reinvent the aptly named polo shirt. First created by René Lacoste and already worn by the likes of JFK, Bing Crosby, and the Duke of Windsor, Lauren took the shirt from a sportswear staple into a casual wear one. The shirt was an immediate hit and soon became an indelible icon of preppy East Coast style. In *Ralph Lauren's Polo Shirt* book, the designer described its immediate success in the introduction, "When I created my Polo shirt in 1972, everyone responded." The designer could only assume, "Maybe it was the way the collar stood up, or the placket, or the excitement of the many colors we made it in."

The designer's decision to make the shirt in various shades was recognized as a key reason for the shirt's success; there were seventeen in 1977, which expanded to more than seventy over time. The color choices—each one chosen by Lauren himself—were just the beginning. The Ralph Lauren polo shirt put quality at the forefront, and was crafted from breathable piqué cotton instead of polyester, which gave it a worn-in, authentic feel. It had the appeal of the polo player emblem (famously created using 1,100 stitches) which made the shirt instantly recognizable now that the logo had moved from the shirt cuff to the left chest. It has become the brand's most well-known piece, and, true to preppy style as a whole, it remains sporty and refined, and with an aspirational quality.

Star Power on Polos

It wasn't long before the Ralph Lauren Polo shirt was worn by Hollywood stars, athletes, rappers, and US presidents. Bill Clinton wore his around the White House; Frank Sinatra famously bought twenty of them in one shopping trip; Leonardo DiCaprio wore one in Martin Scorsese's *The Wolf of Wall Street;* and Chance the Rapper wore the 2013 re-release of the Flag Bear during some of his performances in 2016 and 2017. Star power boosted the appeal of the Polo shirt (and Ralph Lauren as a brand), as well as cementing its cultural significance in American fashion.

Versatile, truly timeless, and cross-generational, it's no wonder this preppy staple has now been permanently included in the Museum of Modern Art's "Items: Is Fashion Modern?" exhibit.

Beyond the Polo

Every once in a while, a film comes along that proves to be a source of sartorial inspiration. In 1974, it was the ultra-stylish adaptation of *The Great Gatsby*—the legendary Jazz-Age tale by F. Scott Fitzgerald that focused on outsiders in pursuit of the American dream. Set in a world of debaucherous mansion parties and feathered flapper girls, it highlighted the debonair East Coast style of the social elite. Creating the distinguished suits of the male cast (including a custom pink one worn by Robert Redford's Jay Gatsby) catapulted Ralph Lauren—an up-and-coming designer at the time—into the limelight. The preppy-inspired outfits won the film an Oscar for costume design and earned the cover shot in *Newsweek*.

It wasn't the only film to help establish Lauren as a major player in Hollywood. He also dressed Diane Keaton in Woody Allen's Oscar-winning 1977 film *Annie Hall*. Similar to era-defining *Gatsby*, the androgynous look worn by Keaton in the role became an unexpected style influence, one that generations of women would emulate. The slouchy high-waisted pants, black waistcoat, and patterned Ralph Lauren tie combination that Keaton wore started a borrowed-from-the-boys trend. It was a nod to the early years of Ivy League style when students from Seven Sisters colleges made it their own by wearing men's Brooks Brothers shirts. Ralph Lauren sales surged after the film's release and, fast-forward to 2016, the designer paid homage to *Annie Hall* with textures of tweed, taupe-hued tailoring, and oversized knitwear for the brand's autumn/winter collection. As American designer Michael Kors once so deftly put it to *GQ* magazine, "Ralph is the ultimate cinematic storyteller and his clothes made movies such as 1974's *The Great Gatsby* and *Annie Hall* unforgettable . . . He's helped take American fashion and turn it into a lifestyle loved all around the world."

A Way of Living

The rise continued for Ralph Lauren, who was single-handedly curating a high-gloss version of all-American style. Consistency was becoming key to his brand's success. With each new season collection released, the core DNA of preppy style always remained the same. Lauren became one of the few designers to stick to what they know, safe in the knowledge that what they do is what they're best at. From relaxed chinos and cabled cashmere sweaters to Hamptons-inspired stripes and pony-clad polo shirts, Lauren was keeping prep relevant and shaping the narrative.

In 1983, Lauren channeled this same aesthetic into interiors with the launch of his Home collection. The stage had already been set by Laura Ashley in the 1950s, but Lauren was still one of the first major fashion designers to really up the ante in the home sphere. His dedication to fashion as a lifestyle, in all its forms, meant it was a natural next step. "The reason I decided to enter home furnishing forty years ago was because I had something to say. I knew I wanted to make as complete a statement for the home as I had with my fashion collections. The Home collection was my way of sharing a complete world—a way to share my vision of living," he said in his 2023 book, *Ralph Lauren A Way of Living: Home, Design, Inspiration.*

From furniture and bed linen to china and wallpaper, the brand's homeware could be used to conceive entire environments. It used the same design references as Ralph Lauren's clothes, mixing prep with bohemian touches and influences from Western, Cowboy culture. Ralph Lauren's first home collection was a timeless rustic-meets-refined look, a style that always feels cozy, comforting, and warm. "Home is where the heart is, and that is where we seek quality and comfort," the designer said. Whether it's an oceanfront house in Montauk decorated with wicker and nautical stripes, the big-city glamour of a Manhattan apartment, or a log cabin in Colorado accented with faux antlers, cowhide rugs, and original Navajo blankets; the aesthetic is instantly identifiable as being Ralph. With *The New York Times* reporting in 1983 that advance store orders for the new Ralph Lauren home-furnishing line was "expected to do from $30 million to $35 million in its first year," it's easy to see why many tried to emulate his success. Lilly Pulitzer, Calvin Klein, Donna Karan, among others, all followed in his footsteps with their own home collections.

A Revolution in Retail

A pioneer in creating an aspirational lifestyle brand, Ralph Lauren expressed preppy style not only through his clothes and homeware, but his retail environments and even his fragrances (the Polo For Men fragrance smells like pine, leather, and tobacco, which according to the brand, evokes "the sight and sound of galloping horses on the freshly cut, green polo field"). The fact Lauren found a way to evolve prep into all aspects of life—right down to scent—highlights his extraordinary ability to sell the perfect fantasy. Ralph Lauren's approach to luxury living has lasted because it allows us to lose ourselves in his romanticized vision of America: leafy Ivy League campuses, manicured Montauk lawns, and antique-adorned Colorado ranches. "I don't design clothes," Lauren once said. "I design dreams."

He became the first American designer to have a freestanding store in Europe when he opened The Polo Shop on London's New Bond Street in 1981, and revolutionized retail further with the first Ralph Lauren flagship in April 1986. Situated within the historic Rhinelander mansion at the corner of Madison Avenue and East 72nd Street in New York City, no expense was spared when it came to the recently refurbished interior. The French Renaissance Revival–style building was adorned with intricately detailed vaulted ceilings, hand-carved mahogany balustrades, marble fireplaces, oak floors, and Persian rugs. There was velvet drapery, green felt walls, period furniture, and antique paintings. It created a lived-in, homely look that was highly curated yet true to Ralph Lauren's form, looking as if it had always been there. The window displays were just as evocative: mannequins in Oxford shirts and repp ties with cable-knit sweaters casually knotted around the shoulders and polished loafers perfectly placed on a wingback chair. Everything about the shopping destination was designed to let the customer experience the world from the Polo point of view.

Launching the flagship was a risky yet trailblazing move. At the time, Ralph Lauren's clothing was only being sold at Bloomingdale's, Saks Fifth Avenue, and a handful of other high-end shops. There were concerns by department stores that Rhinelander would have a negative effect on their Ralph Lauren sales. No other designer before him had attempted to offer men's, women's, and children's clothes in a single space; this kind of total brand experience was new. Lauren said at the time, "This store is the essence of everything I have said since my first necktie. I want this to be more than a store. I'm not just selling clothes. I'm selling a world, a notion of style." That was certainly what it was.

The Polo Mansion, as it became affectionately known, was hugely successful. People flocked there, and it made a huge $100,000 on opening day. In turn, it not only boosted sales in the department stores, but Ralph Lauren's retail space at Bloomingdale's doubled the following year as a result. The mansion fundamentally changed the way Americans shopped and made Ralph Lauren's signature preppy style accessible to everyone.

The Lo Life Crew

As the brand's influence spread, it was unexpectedly adopted by Brooklyn-based street crews as a symbol of status and style in the late '80s. Far removed from the Waspy, country-club types that typically wore Ralph Lauren, these were groups of "underprivileged Black and Latino youths who were growing up" in some of Brooklyn's toughest neighborhoods, listening to hip-hop and known for shoplifting designer clothing. There was Ralphie's Kids from St. John's and Utica in Crown Heights, and U.S.A. (United Shoplifters Association) from Marcus Garvey Village in Brownsville. In 1988, they ditched their respective names and banded together to officially become the Lo Lifes. The moniker came from the last syllable of Polo, and meant that you lived the life of Lo: You were a Polo enthusiast, wearing the clothes and living the lifestyle on the streets. To the Lo Lifes, Ralph Lauren was much more than a designer brand. "We always had a heavy emphasis on 'Lo. It made us exclusive. The colors stood out and people were able to identify us. Polo became a uniform," said rapper and cofounder of the Lo Lifes, Rack-Lo (aka George Billips).

Shoplifting Polo, or "boosting" as it was known, became a badge of honor. The brand came with the biggest social status, so crew members would get their hands on them by any means necessary. They'd hop on trains uptown in droves and head to swanky department stores like Saks Fifth Avenue, Macy's, and Bloomingdale's. Dozens of Lo Lifes would descend onto the shop floor, rushing clothing racks, and clearing them of everything Ralph Lauren—often leaving with armfuls of polo shirts, jeans, rugby shirts, and coats worth thousands of dollars. After all, it wasn't enough to just wear one Ralph Lauren item; Lo Lifes needed to dress head to toe in the brand. The movement was highly competitive, and crew members would return to Brooklyn to rap about the clothing they had stolen. However, wearing the newest Polo pieces had its drawbacks; getting robbed—or sometimes even killed—for them became commonplace.

"People would rob your house. People would shoot you for the shirts," Thirstin Howl III, one of the original Lo Lifers, told *The Guardian*. The most sought-after pieces were bold and bright Ski '92 jackets. "We called that the 'suicide' ski jacket because if you wore that out in the street it was like suicide. You would probably get killed for it," producer Just Blaze told *Complex* in 1992.

Aspiration Gone Astray

How did the Lo Life crew start dressing exclusively in a clothing brand that was so synonymous with the American high life? "Well, it's aspirational clothing. What I mean by that is, you can just look at how Ralph came up . . . he didn't come from a lot of money," Just Blaze said in a *Complex* interview. "A lot of his designs were based on things that he wished he had, things that he aspired to, a certain lifestyle he aspired to live. So I think as time progressed into our generation, it's kind of the same thing."

The brand's preppy fashion, once the domain of affluent, white students on the campuses of East Coast private schools, were now being worn in some of the most dangerous areas in Brooklyn. Far removed from the early days of Princeton and Palm Beach, the flag-embroidered baseball caps, striped polos, and sporty red tracksuits of Ivy League–inspired style contrasted greatly with the surroundings. "It wasn't worn by people who lived in our community," Rack-Lo said about the brand. "Polo was made for the rich, Waspy kids; it wasn't made for urban kids."

Ralph Lauren's American dream was never intended for the likes of the Lo Life crew, but they decided to take it anyway, appropriate it, and make it their own. The Lo Lifes wanted better for themselves, and clothing was the way to do it. "When we would come back to our neighborhoods wearing these clothes, you looked like somebody. You felt like somebody," said Howl in HBO's 2019 documentary *Very Ralph*. "And if you managed to wear Polo on the streets—and not get it stolen off your back—it was an added badge of honor." It wasn't all about aspiration though. The vibrant colors and designs of the Polo brand were appreciated by the Lo Lifes, who styled it in a way that made them stand out. Considered to be the first street-style stars, they were throwing the newest pieces together and getting photographed outside clubs and events—even by those outside the subculture. It resulted in a one-upmanship, as those in the community competed to create the coolest looks.

By the beginning of the '90s, many of the original Lo Lifes were in jail, dead, or had moved away. While the Lo Life subculture may have faded from the mainstream, the fashion remained with the younger generations, and a whole host of labels continue to reference the aesthetic—one brand, in particular, was Supreme. A successful brand speaks to people wherever they are, not just to a targeted demographic; and that's exactly what Ralph Lauren managed to do with his Polo Sport line. "I don't know why, but they got it," Lauren said of the Lo Lifers. "They understood the purity of my vision." The influence Lo Life subculture had on Ralph Lauren and preppy style was the catalyst to both becoming an established part of hip-hop culture in the years that followed.

The American Dream

What started as a humble tie-selling business has grown into a multibillion-dollar empire that's as woven into the fabric of American culture as stars and stripes. The reason for Ralph Lauren's success? He's one of the few designers who doesn't follow fashion trends, choosing instead to focus on cultivating classic pieces that endure. "Style is very personal," is how Lauren put it. "It has nothing to do with fashion. Fashion is over quickly. Style is forever." Timelessness is partly why the brand has remained popular for almost five decades. At its core, however, is the fact that Ralph Lauren has only ever really sold one thing: his own vision of the American Dream.

Inspired by the Ivy League, country clubs, and Midwestern ranches, he single-handedly manufactured the idea of an aspirational all-American lifestyle. He then marketed it back to the WASPs who initially inspired him, Brooklyn-based street gangs in the '80s, as well as everyone in-between. The brand made preppy style versatile enough for everyone to wear (or decorate with), and everyone wanted to be a part of it. This all came from the man who once said, "I don't design clothes; I design dreams."

"Ralph Lauren sells much more than fashion. He sells the life you'd like to lead," Oprah Winfrey said simply and directly. "To own a creation of Ralph Lauren's is to savor a taste of the American dream. He has elevated what Americans see as possible for ourselves by offering a snapshot of a storybook lifestyle that somehow feels attainable."

It's easy to forget just how remarkable Ralph Lauren is when long-lasting success in the industry is rare. With an unwavering consistency to his vision and a reluctance to follow the market, Lauren has emerged as a mainstay. It's therefore little surprise that he's the first designer to win all the Council of Fashion Designers of America's highest honors: the Lifetime Achievement Award, which was presented to him by muse and close friend Audrey Hepburn in 1992. Add to that his very own bronze plaque embedded into the sidewalk on New York's Fashion Walk of Fame, which showcases his commitment to "interpreting classic American style," drawing on "every important look in this country's clothing history." Many brands wouldn't exist without Ralph leading the way.

After defining American fashion for decades, the designer stepped down as CEO in 2015, but the preppy country-club look continues to reign supreme at the company. After all, when it comes to marketing prep as a style that's strong and easily recognizable, Ralph Lauren did it first.

The Preppy Boom

At the tail end of the '70s and throughout the '80s, prep reached its height. From classic movies that changed the whole vernacular of the style to an in-depth handbook that carefully detailed (albeit in a lighthearted way) all the rules you needed to follow if you wanted to be preppy, clothing that was once a sign of privilege had shifted to be made for the masses. Brooke Shields, wearing high-waisted blue jeans and a pink polo with a yellow sweater draped around her shoulders, alongside Princess Diana in polo outfits consisting of a blazer, sweatshirt, jeans, and a baseball cap, were certainly the preppy looks of the decade.

A *Love Story*

As Ivy League style adapted and evolved, so did its name. It was first dubbed "Ivy League" because, quite literally, it was clothing that was popularized on the campuses of elite colleges. However, this uniform of class and wealth—and not to mention wannabe class and wealth—soon became known as something else, with the credit largely due to the cult 1970 movie *Love Story*. Telling the tale of the doomed Ivy League romance between blue-blooded Harvard jock Oliver and Radcliffe College coed Jenny (played by Ryan O'Neal and Ali MacGraw), the movie not only amplified preppy style, but introduced the term "preppy" itself into the lexicon. Although it was a term bandied around for years, when Ali MacGraw's character, Jenny, affectionately teases Oliver about his privileged upbringing by calling him "preppy," it was its first major use in popular culture.

The term stuck. Forget calling somebody "Ivy League" because they wore button-downs and natural-shouldered jackets; from the '70s and '80s onward, Ivy League became outdated, and it was now all about being preppy.

Cinematic Influence

As well as popularizing the term, the hit *Love Story*—earning $107 million during its initial release—captured preppy style in nearly every scene. From the romantic snowstorm to all the heart-to-hearts set against the Barrett Hall backdrop, the movie was shot mostly at Harvard (every year incoming freshmen get treated to a *Love Story* screening as a result) and was a definitive textbook on preppy style. Think striped repp ties, tennis sweaters, Oxford shoes, not forgetting the inimitable combination of red tights and a tartan skirt made iconic by MacGraw's character as she was carried over the threshold. *Love Story* still influences the fall collections of fashion designers over half a century later, Michael Kors, Tommy Hilfiger, and Emilia Wickstead to name a few.

Are You a Preppie?

In the decade that followed, thanks largely to Ralph Lauren and *Love Story*'s influence, Ivy had truly given way to prep (ironically, Brooks Brothers famously disliked being referred to as prep). But it wasn't just the terminology that had changed. The style had evolved into a casual, Americanized look that was much more consciously copied than its predecessor. Preppy was also more open to derision than Ivy. Dorm rooms were adorned with the instantly recognizable 1979 "Are You a Preppie?" poster by Tom Shadyac. It was designed and printed by the director (his movies include *Patch Adams, Ace Ventura: Pet Detective*, and *Liar, Liar*) when he was a student at the University of Virginia as a way to fundraise for his fraternity.

Showing a chino-clad, hands-on-hips prep with a tick-box outfit labeled with a "navy blah blazer," "horn-rim glasses" and "smirk optional," the poster ended up being incredibly popular. At this point, everyone could spot a prep, and this humorous interpretation of a stereotype became an important touchstone in preppy history With lines like, "Do you dress in a way that attracts women to other men?" and "At your college football games, do you dress like a neon sign?" the playful poster defined a generation of college students. It also inspired countless tributes, one of which occurred nearly forty years later when Rowing Blazers paid homage to the poster by collaborating with Tom Shadyac on a sell-out capsule collection of T-shirts and hoodies emblazoned with the iconic design.

Lessons from the *Handbook*

Lisa Birnbach's *The Official Preppy Handbook* was another case in point. Hitting bookstore shelves in October 1980, the tongue-in-cheek guide was originally written as a satirical take on successfully navigating the preppy life but ended up creating a cultural moment that introduced millions to the style. Its authors explain how the book will teach you "to be really top drawer," from nicknames (after all, it gives a certain in-ness and inaccessibility to others) to dressing the part (just don't wear black, and collars, if possible, are always turned up).

Much of the *Handbook*'s most useful advice came in the fashion section, which combined knowingness with a witty twist. When it comes to choosing a classic shirt, for example, it has to be a "Brooks Brothers button-down all-cotton Oxford cloth shirt." The color? Pink, and "no one except Brooks has ever been able to achieve that perfect pink or roll to the collar." There was an eye for detail that helped new preppies know everything they needed to know; from the one fabric that was quintessentially preppy (true madras, of course), when not to wear socks and what you should (and shouldn't) monogram. A year later, after Birnbach's book was launched, prep's popularity at the time meant it was still on *The New York Times* Best Seller list. The now-classic but out-of-print book sold more than a million copies—according to *The New York Times*—and was reprinted a huge thirty-two times before publication ended in 1995.

Prep in the Press

Just like the *Handbook*, preppy style was everywhere. Everyone was seeing and talking about it, including the media. There was plenty of coverage in the newspapers showing the shifting trend in fashion toward the style. In a 1980 article from *Time* magazine, a saleswoman at a high-fashion shoe store, Pella, in Atlanta's Lenox Square, was asked about the burgeoning preppy style in America. She replied, "If one more person comes in here and asks for Bass Weejuns, I think I'll scream." It's no surprise those new to preppy style were after G.H. Bass & Co.'s penny loafers; they've been worn by the likes of JFK, Audrey Hepburn, Grace Kelly, and Paul Newman since they debuted back in 1936. And when, in 1982, Michael Jackson donned a pair of black Weejuns in his "Thriller" video (albeit while breaking the rules by wearing them with white socks, no less) it only amplified how much preppy style had gone mainstream.

In the same *Time* article, called "Here Comes the Preppie Look," it covered the change in aesthetic. Opening with "Fashion goes back to school, with a flair," the article goes on to highlight that "snappy blue blazers and tweed hacking jackets, button-down Oxford-cloth shirts and Shetland sweaters, khaki slacks, and tartan skirts" were now all in. The writer commented how, "This summer and fall, the fashion-conscious woman will be wearing exactly what the fashion-unconscious woman has been wearing for decades. It is currently labeled the Preppie Look, though the style has also been known as Ivy League, Town and Country, Brooks Brothers or—in England—County." And even back in 1980, prep's timelessness was realized: "Many fashion experts point out that the basic appeal of Preppiana is that they are 'investment clothes.'" Press coverage at this time created more buzz around prep and amplified the style further by allowing it to spread quickly, but there's no doubt the trend already existed for years.

The Rise and Fall of J.Crew

Fueled by the success of *Love Story* and *The Official Preppy Handbook*, preppy style's international appeal in the 1980s was at its peak. This, paired with the popularity of Ralph Lauren, paved the way for J.Crew. The company, initially known as Popular Sale Club, was founded by Mitchell Cinader and Saul Charles in 1947 as a door-to-door business that sold low-priced womenswear. It was relaunched in 1983 by Arthur Cinader (the founder's son) as a mail-order retailer, who named it J.Crew. Inspired by Ralph Lauren's Polo label, Cinader picked Crew, in a nod to campus oarsmen, and then added the initial J—borrowed from Ivy League atelier J. Press—to add a similar aspirational quality.

He aimed to provide a cheaper alternative to Ralph Lauren; something that was more stylish than other mail-order brands already out there, such as Lands' End or L.L.Bean. But unlike Ralph with its ubiquitous pony or Lacoste's green crocodile, J.Crew focused less on distinguishable logos and more on adopting an understated, insider appeal. It was classic, timeless fashion: a lineup of tailored suits, white button-down shirts (a true prep staple), and a range of quietly luxurious accessories. All sold—at the beginning anyway—through an iconic catalog that became a recognizable part of the brand's identity (so much so it was brought back for the Fall 2024 campaign). The brand not only defined the American prep aesthetic, but successfully created a line that served as the gateway into J.Crew's preppy world. It was a world where access was everything; you had to be invited in. J.Crew established a loyal following by delivering it to the mailboxes of over three million potential customers; the founder and then-chairman Arthur Cinader told *The New York Times* that twelve thousand were distributed on Manhattan's Upper East Side alone. It would go on to become a cultural phenomenon.

Affordable Prep

It wasn't Arthur Cinader's dream to become the next Ralph Lauren. He had no real interest in fashion and no experience of Ivy League (Cinader attended public schools and a state college), but he wanted to keep the family business he inherited from his father as profitable as possible. Launching J.Crew was a calculated bid to do exactly that. It was created to meet the increasing demand for both preppy style and mail-order catalogs, especially those who loved Ralph Lauren's polos, cable knits, and chinos, but couldn't quite meet Lauren's price point. To earn credibility with fans of Ivy League, Cinader made false claims that the original J.Crew was a men's haberdashery in Princeton. It imitated the respected, long-standing appeal of old-line brands like Brooks Brothers and J. Press, and even stated in the first catalog, "The heritage of J.Crew weekend clothes is 100 years of outfitting rugby, lacrosse, and crew." In fact, the company attached a J.Crew label to existing designs from manufacturers and was based out of a New Jersey warehouse. But it didn't seem to really matter; the brand's apparel was selling.

Cinader struck upon "affordable prep" at just the right time. Despite being told that most successful mail-order companies were running at a deficit until two and a half years after launch, J.Crew broke even roughly eighteen months later. The start-up was gathering momentum, and not long after the first J.Crew catalog (which was shot at Harvard's Weld Boathouse) was sent out, telephone operators were struggling to keep up with the sheer number of calls from customers wanting to place orders. The only problem was that J.Crew catalogs still didn't look hugely different to that of Lands' End.

It was Emily Cinader, Arthur's daughter, who joined her father's company—fresh out of a marketing degree at the University of Denver as an enigmatic twenty-one-year-old. She had firsthand experience of the preppy lifestyle that J.Crew wanted to embody and decided to take the catalogs in a different creative direction. With her input, the fledgling brand was supercharged.

Delivered to Your Door

Before the days of shopping almost exclusively on phones through websites, apps, or social media, dressing preppy meant ordering from a physical magazine via phone or filling in an order form—and that's exactly how thousands of dedicated American shoppers once got their J.Crew. The brand jumped on the mail-order boom days of the '80s, which was largely thanks to the rise of career women. After all, working a nine-to-five left little time for browsing department stores, but a catalog could be looked at anytime and anywhere.

Now carefully curated by Emily Cinader, the arrival of the glossy J.Crew catalog was a much-anticipated event. Many would pour through the pages and circle the clothes they wanted as soon as the catalog arrived. The thirteen annual editions became key to the success of J.Crew's early years. Each one carefully detailed how to dress—always loose and relaxed—and how to live—preferably by the beach, on the East Coast. In every copy, styling was approached as storytelling and depicted a glamorous, picturesque, and easygoing American lifestyle. While traditional catalogs simply highlighted the product, Cinader used editorial-worthy photography to place the clothes in a fictional universe of wholesome, preppy outdoorsiness. The aim was to make a catalog that didn't feel like a catalog. One that breathed life into J.Crew's timeless clothing and looked just as beautiful as pictures that graced the pages of fashion magazines like *Vogue*.

Using "lifestyle photography" in catalogs wasn't new. After all, Ralph Lauren had got there first with his striking ad campaigns that were pinned to many a dorm room wall. Lauren had already changed the game by showcasing his collections exactly where you'd expect the East Coast elite to be: stately homes, golf greens, and on yachts. But Lauren's models never looked like they were having much fun. That's where J.Crew was different. Positioning itself as a brand that wasn't just more affordable, but also more real, Cinader aimed to create a clothing catalog that didn't feel forced or inauthentic, and she achieved it.

Marketed to the Masses

For its first couple of years, J.Crew had no design team. Apart from customizing the color, adding a J.Crew label, and sometimes the odd button or two, most of the understated pieces sold by the brand were standard designs from private-label manufacturers. Cinader attempted to elevate the product range by bringing in things to copy—whether it was an entire style from another brand or just imitating a certain detail or color. It would then be sent off and returned as a J.Crew product. Some of J.Crew's most iconic pieces were subtle reinterpretations of existing items.

Take the brand's instantly recognizable anorak; it was based on an old sailing jacket that Cinader remembered her father wearing when she was little. Another hallmark piece, the roll-neck sweater from 1988 was inspired by an old woolen pullover that Cinader's ex-boyfriend had inherited from his grandfather.

In 1985, designer Linda Snyder was hired, and the company's first sample room soon followed, with a real J.Crew design team starting to take shape. The brand's pared-back, preppy aesthetic of striped tees, ruffled blouses, chinos, sweaters, and striped rugby shirts soon appealed to the masses. J.Crew was selling easy-to-wear Americana, and there were plenty eager to buy it—sales increased from $3 million to $100 million in the 1980s.

"Real" Models

J.Crew models were classically beautiful, rather than being intimidatingly so, and the same regular cast of "characters" would return with each new catalog for added familiarity (as a result, J.Crew catalog models became so recognizable during the '80s they ended up having legions of fans). There was a nonchalance to the styling—untucked shirts, rolled-up sleeves, and sweaters knotted around the waist—which made the brand's look seem achievable. Keen to avoid models from looking like "catalog people" who were solely there to sell you things, Cinader made sure they were *always* in motion. The catalog's pages were brimming with snapshots of everything from al fresco meals in the Hamptons to laughing, piggybacking couples in Newport, and friends riding tandem on bicycles on Harbor Island. Wearing anoraks, chambray shirts, or classic roll-neck sweaters while doing so, you could count on J.Crew for effortless style no matter the setting. By the '90s, catalog editors and staff would check for any signs of "fakery" before it went to print.

The First J.Crew Store

Although it was a potentially risky move for a business built on the back of a carefully curated mail-order catalog, Arthur Cinader opened J.Crew's first brick-and-mortar store in March 1989. The brand already had a loyal following from its catalog business, and the aim was now to reach customers who shopped in an entirely different way. The flagship location in the South Street Seaport in Manhattan wasn't chosen on a whim; it was carefully selected based on catalog data. The historic area was popular with tourists and close enough to Wall Street to allow for after-work shopping. When it came to expanding to Boston, the Chestnut Hill Mall, which was close to at least a dozen colleges, was a no-brainer. "We never meet a college student who doesn't know J.Crew very well," Arthur Cinader once said.

Just like the practical style tips that peppered the catalog's pages, J.Crew became a place where you could learn how to dress preppy. Its stores offered a more relaxed alternative to the formal settings of Brooks Brothers or J. Press, and there were many knowledgeable staff dotted around the shop floor who could not only help you buy something but also offer advice on how to wear it.

At this point, the brand had successfully infiltrated culture. It makes sense, then, that J.Crew was now the one being imitated. Where it had first gained popularity marketing itself as an affordable alternative to Ralph Lauren, now there were fashion labels offering themselves as a less expensive version of J.Crew, including Gap, Abercrombie & Fitch, Banana Republic, and Old Navy. Even its mail-order catalogs were copied.

Boom Days Are Over

The golden days of mail-order catalogs started to slow. Once a staple for brand marketing, companies were beginning to ditch catalogs in favor of digital marketing. By 1990, *The New York Times* headlined an article, "Even for J.Crew, the mail-order boom days are over." J.Crew managed to weather the downturn thanks to its traditional brick-and-mortar stores; but it wasn't the only challenge the brand faced. The popularity of prep waxed and waned since its '80s heyday, and during the mid to late '90s, the grunge scene—with its baggy jeans, oversized jackets, plaid shirts, and beaten-up Converse—was edging out the style. Trying to keep up, J.Crew struggled to decide which direction to take and stepped away from its signature casual and outdoorsy look (albeit briefly).

According to J.Crew's website, the 1990s were "A decade of versatility: when anoraks were tops and a button-up could be a beach cover-up." But it was also when Abercrombie & Fitch and its youthful, trendy interpretation of prep (along with the shirtless models that were stationed outside its flagship stores) caught the eye of some of J.Crew's younger demographic. By the late '90s and early 2000s, Abercrombie & Fitch's upturned-collar polos, striped graphic tees, and logo-detailed hoodies meant J.Crew's more classic aesthetic just wasn't "cool." Profit margins tanked.

Comeback Crew

From the mid-2000s to the mid-2010s, J.Crew (joined by the likes of Abercrombie and Gap) dominated malls. The brand was riding high under the direction of Jenna Lyons—who was something of a cultural icon in the fashion industry—and CEO Mickey Drexler, known in retail as "The Merchant Prince" who turned around the Gap. Lyons was first hired by J.Crew in 1990 at the age of twenty-one and fresh out of Parsons School of Design, before working her way up. Once at the top, she reinvented the brand's preppy aesthetic with designs that were deemed by some as being too high-fashion and, at times, too sequin-laden. Drexler, on the other hand, was busy upping prices and limiting quantities to create demand. A simple cashmere tee came with a $188 price tag, and in 2008, a "J.Crew Collection" sweater was priced at an eye-watering $1,900—in the middle of a recession, no less. At the same time, the menswear side of the business was beginning to flourish. Made with luxurious Loro Piana wool, J.Crew's ubiquitous slim-fitting Ludlow suit was introduced the same year and had instant appeal. Sales of men's suits doubled at J.Crew after it was launched and remained an iconic piece.

The brand reached a pivotal moment in 2008 when First Lady Michelle Obama wore green J.Crew gloves to her husband's first inauguration (and a bold bejeweled belt at the second). The brand's website crashed the following day from the volume of traffic. Over the years, Obama made J.Crew her relatable uniform—there were argyle sweaters, turquoise coats, ruffled blouses, tweed pencil skirts, and many, many cardigans. Preppy style has long been associated with American presidents—JFK famously loved his Ralph Lauren polos and Abraham Lincoln had a Brooks Brothers coat intricately embroidered with an eagle and the inscription, "One Country, One Destiny"—and J.Crew had joined the prestigious ranks. J.Crew had finally become what Arthur Cinader had started out pretending to be when he embellished the brand's Princeton origins all those years ago: an American brand with real heritage.

Identity Crisis

Lyons continued to move away from the code of effortless, all-day dressing that the brand had so effectively cracked, by securing its very own slot on the official show calendar of New York Fashion Week in 2011. Commenting on its debut at the time, a *Vogue* article said, "In the last six or so years, J.Crew has gone from preppy brand with a beautifully shot catalog to a quirkily preppy brand with a beautifully shot catalog and a significant voice in the conversation on American style."

But as one blogger put it in 2015 with a post called, "Do you still heart J.Crew?" it claimed J.Crew seemed to be "catering to the fashion editors and fashionistas from Fashion Week more than the base of loyal aficionadas." It's true that in Drexler and Lyons' first ten years together, the brand's revenue tripled. However, by 2014, the company was suffering an identity crisis. The daring, post-prep aesthetic was failing, and it was criticized for no longer reflecting its roots. It was also becoming more expensive and exclusive, without the quality and perfect fit to match, and so J.Crew loyalists left in droves.

J.Crew's debts were mounting as a result, their sales continued to decline, and creative director and president Jenna Lyons departed in 2017. Mickey Drexler told *The Wall Street Journal* that exclusivity became the company's biggest flaw, saying, "We became a little too elitist in our attitude," and "We gave a perception of being a higher-priced company than we were—in our catalog, online, and in our general presentation."

On top of this, the catalog, a beloved icon of American fashion for three decades, was discontinued in 2017. J.Crew, once a go-to for prep-inspired wardrobe basics, finally buckled under risky stylistic decisions and the weight of $1.65 billion corporate debt. It was one of the first major retailers to file for bankruptcy in 2020 in the early days of the pandemic.

The (Near) Fall

There was the assumption that the bankruptcy filing would spell the end of J.Crew, but with a $400 million line of credit put forward by investors to fund a restoration effort, the brand's legacy was saved. From the days of elaborate catalog photo shoots that epitomized wealthy Americana, through to the Michelle Obama–era of signature button-up cardigans and the famed Jenna Lyons years, the brand has played a part in channeling New England coastal cool into the broader conversation of style and culture.

J.Crew borrowed from Ralph Lauren's already tried-and-tested method, selling a lifestyle in which it would best exist. Over the last forty years, the preppy style that Arthur Cinader wanted to mass-market has been defined and redefined many times and J.Crew has tried—sometimes with great success—to keep up. So much so, its fingerprints remain all over the preppy scene today.

Preppy Is Everywhere

Back to the '90s when J.Crew was still doing what it did best—clean-cut, easy Americana that was affordable and cool—prep fashion was being embraced by an audience outside of its typical Ivy League–educated enthusiasts. By this point, the style had exploded well beyond its elitist past. Brands like Tommy Hilfiger became ubiquitous in the hip-hop world. *Clueless* helped kick off a new wave of preppy minimalism with its iconic fashion moments. Princess Diana was pictured trying to avoid the paparazzi in a cowl-neck Harvard sweatshirt (so pivotal that the costume department of *The Crown* asked the Ivy League university to recreate it for Season 5 of the series). Then there was Carlton Banks in the sitcom *The Fresh Prince of Bel-Air*, an unlikely style icon known for his Waspy wardrobe of V-neck sweaters, ties, and chinos. All these—among many other touchpoints—meant prep was everywhere.

The Influence of Hip-Hop

As hip-hop evolved, so did preppy style. The Lo Lifes had set hip-hop's love affair with prep fashion in motion, and its inclusion in the ever-growing culture continued through to the mid-'90s. Dressing head to toe in Ralph Lauren's Polo Sport line had become commonplace with the "boosting" crews of New York City, and now rappers in collegiate sweaters were dropping the names of other designer labels to signify status.

In 1992, Grand Puba, a member of the hip-hop group Brand Nubian, introduced a brand that (although it had been founded seven years earlier) was new to the hip-hop community: Tommy Hilfiger. Dressed in a color-blocked Polo Ralph Lauren Alpine rugby shirt, he gave a shout-out to prep when he mentioned wearing "Tommy Hilfiger top gear" on the 1992 track, "What's the 411?" Hilfiger recognized the potential buying power of hip-hop culture early, giving the rapper thousands of dollars of free clothes in response and offering more for any future music videos or photo shoots. It was an innovative move—especially at a time when gifting clothes to promote brands was relatively unheard of—and pioneered the music merchandise game. This was the decade where hip-hop artists embraced preppy brands, and many of those same brands embraced them in turn.

Cosigning Tommy Hilfiger

Whether it was getting Aaliyah and DJ Mark Ronson to pose in a 1996 Hilfiger campaign or dressing Snoop Dogg in a Tommy Hilfiger rugby shirt to perform on *Saturday Night Live* in 1994, Hilfiger realized getting cool people to wear his clothes raised his—and as a result, prep's—profile. His effortlessly cool lineup of collegiate pieces—signature varsity jackets and polos given a twist with bright graphics, colors, and logos—weren't initially intended for rappers, but soon became a go-to for those in the hip-hop scene, Biggie Smalls, Tupac, and A Tribe Called Quest included.

Recalling the early days of his brand, Tommy Hilfiger told Hypebeast, "Of course, Ralph Lauren and Brooks Brothers were preppy, but I wanted my preppy to be different and cool." He went on to say, "From the very beginning I was making oversized garments and found that a different vibe came from people wearing something more relaxed, versus something that was uptight and a little too aristocratic looking. Mine's always been more for the street." The brand became more ingrained with hip-hop culture as Hilfiger took a sportier, street-influenced approach to his typically classic, all-American style. Everything became oversized, with big logos the norm. Hilfiger explained, "When I redesigned prep in 1985, it was disruptive due to the introduction of oversized, relaxed silhouettes, a stark contrast to the structured preppy look of the time." The designer added, "Each decade has its own unique take on prep style."

For hip-hop stars wearing preppy American brands like Ralph Lauren and Tommy Hilfiger, it was about more than looking fresh. Just as the style had played a role in the Civil Rights Movement of the '50s and '60s, donning styles associated with wealthy white people meant hip-hop artists continued to break down preconceived notions around who was allowed to wear certain clothing based on race. Once exclusionary, the aesthetic was now worn by Black artists in music videos and modeled by them on billboards. This influence on preppy style had created something far cooler and far more inclusive than it had been before. "The original preppy style was something more elite," Hilfiger told GQ in 2022. "[But] right from the start, my intention for the brand was to create style that is accessible to everyone." In fact, Hilfiger's brand only caught the eye of the actual privileged elites once the hip-hop community started to wear it.

Rapper's Delight

Hilfiger played his part in making it more accessible, but there was still an aspirational aspect to his clothing in the early '90s that gave the hip-hop crowd the status upgrade they wanted. Wearing a T-shirt emblazoned with the recognizable red, white, and blue design gave the appearance of wealth and affluence. Hilfiger explained to *The Guardian* why his brand was so popular: "The clothes were very inspired by yachting, prep schools, Ivy League, and New England, where more aristocratic privileged Americans lived and summered in Cape Cod, Nantucket, and the Hamptons. It was actually Russell Simmons, who really is one of the godfathers of hip-hop, who said to me that young street kids and rappers wanted to wear the clothes because they wanted to look rich." At the same time, Hilfiger still wanted to make sure that those who were actually rich knew the brand was for them too. He created dual appeal with campaigns featuring the likes of James and Elizabeth Jagger, Ivanka Trump, and his own children.

In 1996, the unlikely partnership between hip hop and Tommy Hilfiger came to an abrupt end. Unfounded accusations circulated online that Hilfiger had appeared on *The Oprah Winfrey Show* and made racist remarks about the people buying his clothing. Despite Hilfiger being one of the most successful American designers of the '90s, the controversy damaged the brand and his relationship to the music genre. The hip-hop community sidelined Tommy Hilfiger and then began to shift away from preppy style in general. Once hip-hop artists proved preppy was penetrable, it no longer cut it. Rap went luxe, with artists looking to high-octane, high-end designers like Versace and flashy jewelry—often diamond-encrusted, custom-made, and costing thousands of dollars—as an ostentatious reminder of wealth instead.

Ralph's Iconic Snow Beach

Just like its designer-rival Tommy Hilfiger, Ralph Lauren's traditionally preppy aesthetic was intertwined with the hip-hop narrative. By the early to mid-'90s, the culture had served as a free marketing tool for the brand for years. Timeless staples such as polo shirts and cashmere sweaters remained popular with the country-club crowd, but Ralph Lauren started to take a more logo-heavy approach to some of its collegiate classics to match the demand for streetwear.

Ralph Lauren's Polo Sport Snow Beach collection, which hit shelves in the winter of 1993, was aimed at the sporting enthusiasts of a new generation. It consisted of bright, graphic-print technical pieces: hats, hoodies, and a now-iconic pullover jacket in yellow, navy blue, and red. The jacket was worn by Raekwon of the Wu-Tang Clan in the 1994 video for "Can It Be All So Simple," which hyped up demand even more. "When I seen that jacket, the first thing I thought about was, 'Yo this ain't something I seen before,'" Raekwon told *Complex* magazine in 2015. "I was always a fan of Polo, but when I seen that, I felt like I was the only one who had it. So I jumped on it and wore it in the video. Next thing you know, the jacket became famous."

The rapper explained the appeal to *GQ* in 2018: "Polo was the sporty, young-guy type of clothing brand. And people wanted it 'cause it cost a decent amount of money, and people with money wore it. We just adopted it because of the colors, the flags on it." He added, "They were winning back then 'cause they had the university type of feel that everyone loved. All it took was people in the rap game to start talking about it and wear it casually to help the brand climb to a level where they won't even acknowledge it."

The Snow Beach jacket is still deemed one of the rarest, most-coveted styles by Ralph Lauren collectors, and is so sought-after that it can

now go for thousands of dollars when it comes up for resale—with one marketed on eBay for $4,800. The collection's cult appeal is largely down to being limited edition to begin with, but also because the instantly recognizable (for those in the know) designs helped define the era. A new version of prep was ushered in—one that spoke to the hip-hop scene, snowboarders, and street style. Preppiness, in all its forms, transcended fashion to become the fabric of people's lives, no matter where they came from.

Prepping from Philly

While prep was never "out" of style, there's no doubt that it was definitely "in" during the '90s. Rappers were nothing short of Tommy-obsessed. Even Ralph Lauren, known for its classic American style, embraced bold prints and color-blocking with its Polo Sport line. Brands were offering up an edgier take on preppy style, taking classic shapes and twisting them into something contemporary. Once it had successfully infiltrated hip-hop culture, preppy style worked its way into the music mainstream. The who's who of entertainment became a part of the '90s preppy revolution: Britney Spears, TLC, Destiny's Child, Mary J. Blige, and Usher—to name just a few. Prep staples were now just as likely to be seen paired with light-washed Levi's, bucket hats, and the latest Nike Air Force 1 sneakers on the streets of the Bronx as they were with a pair of Sperry Topsiders on holidays in the Hamptons. However, Boyz II Men served as a bridge between the two.

The American vocal harmony group from Philadelphia was known for delivering a string of emotional ballads and hit a cappella harmonies (the quartet's "End of the Road" track reached number one on the *Billboard* Hot 100 for a huge thirteen weeks). Whatever image springs to mind when you think about Boyz II Men, chances are that signature preppy outfits have something to do with it. Any picture of the quartet in the '90s shows them (usually dressed identically) in outfits such as red three-button Brooks Brothers blazers, ties, tennis sweaters, Oxfords, chinos, and of course, baseball caps. They were outfits that made them look as if they'd just stepped out of the coolest Ivy League college in the world. A profile by *Spin* in 1992 even dubbed the group's outfits their "trademark collegiate duds." Boyz II Men member Shawn Stockman told the magazine, "We weren't really into it at first, but once we started wearing the stuff and learning how to put it together, it started to feel good." Boyz II Men elevated the dress code and made it their own, but unlike Tommy and Ralph who were making more obvious tweaks to the aesthetic, they did it without straying too far from the traditional preppy look.

Preppy Pop Culture Moments

Pop culture and fashion have been shaping and influencing each other for years. It's no surprise then that there were plenty of preppy pop culture moments to draw from in the late '90s and '00s. There was Cher Horowitz's enviable wardrobe filled with plaid skirts, Oxford shirts, and sweater vests in the cult classic *Clueless* that are just as relevant today as they were back in 1995. Later, the 1999 film *The Talented Mr. Ripley*, starring Matt Damon and Jude Law, explored the aspirational nature of preppy dressing—Damon's character is mistaken for a wealthy man simply because of the navy blazer (with the Princeton crest) he wears. It's the year that also brought Britney Spears's shrunken twist on prep, with her white knotted button-down and pleated skirt, in her "... Baby One More Time" music video.

While preppy definitely gave way to grunge for a period of the '90s, the style was still there. It made frequent appearances in movies, TV shows, and pop culture throughout the aughts and beyond—and continued to be interpreted and worn in different ways. *Gossip Girl*, which aired from 2007 to 2012, centered around the scandalous, soapy lifestyles of privileged Upper East Side New York teenagers and contrasted with their clean-cut, prep-inspired looks. Indie band Vampire Weekend, who debuted in 2008, caused controversy around glorifying wealth with their take on the traditional preppy look. The band's singer, Ezra Koenig, discussed the origins of their relationship to the "preppy" tag with *Exclaim!* magazine in 2013. "The fact that people freaked out so much at the time also confirmed my feeling that there was something inherently interesting or worthwhile about riffing on preppy clothes and money." Koenig went on to say how, "The whole idea of Vampire Weekend in the beginning was to be a preppy band, but one thing I didn't realize was that, for me, preppy-ness was funny and weird, a bit of a costume."

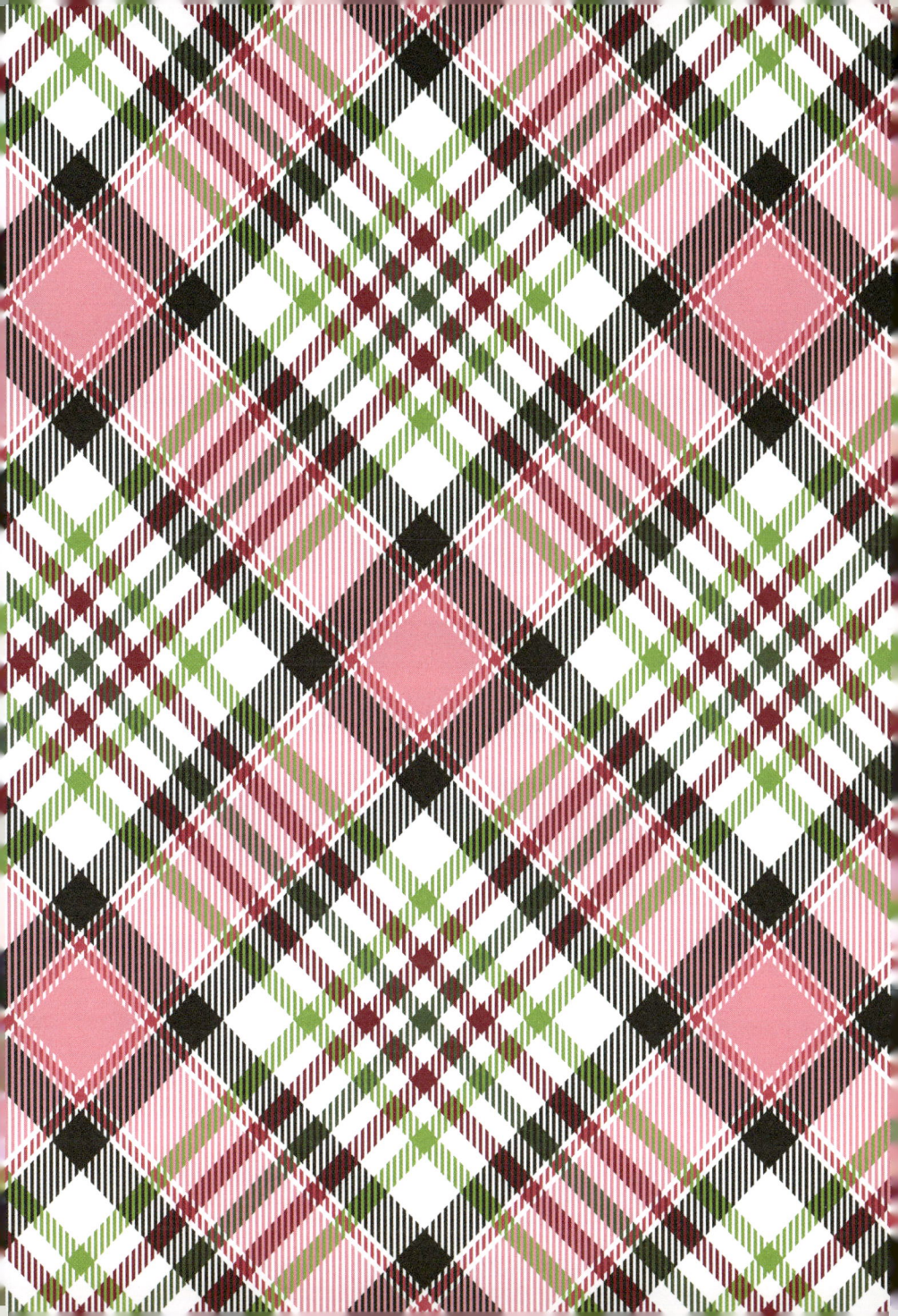

4

Prep Essentials

From its rise in the wood-paneled libraries and boathouses of Ivy League campuses to regular revivals in modern fashion, it's evident that preppy dressing has never truly gone out of style.

The aesthetic, though classic, has learned to adapt and evolve with the times. It's one reason why prep has introduced so many timeless staples throughout the years. From fundamentals like blazers and penny loafers, to striped rugby knits, tennis skirts, and varsity jackets, the most iconic pieces of preppy clothing transcend trend cycles. Some have even become so ubiquitous that they no longer read as preppy and instead are considered everyday "basics," such as button-down shirts and chinos. Of course, it's not just shoes, accessories, and clothing but also patterns and fabrics—ranging from argyle, plaid, seersucker, and cable knit—that also fall under the larger umbrella of preppy.

Polo Shirt

Polo shirts are, without a doubt, the anchor of a preppy wardrobe—most of which are likely to include one or two (at the very least). Defined by its soft collar, short sleeves, and subtly textured piqué-cotton, the polo shirt traces its roots back to the mid-1920s. French tennis player René Lacoste needed a comfortable alternative to the tennis whites of the day, which consisted of a restrictive white long-sleeved shirt, often with a tie, and flannel pants. He took inspiration from tops worn by polo players and designed a similar one for himself that provided improved freedom of movement on the court. It was such a success that the polo shirt became the uniform for all competing players.

Fast forward to 1951, when American manufacturer IZOD gained a license to produce and sell Lacoste shirts in the United States. The brand's inimitable crocodile emblem soon resonated with Ivy Leaguers. However, the polo shirt's assimilation into preppy style can largely be attributed to Ralph Lauren, who launched his iteration in 1972. Coming in a variety of colors and aptly marketed with the tagline "it gets better with age," Ralph Lauren's best-selling polo shirts have remained a constant of American style for over fifty years. Proving that, in terms of preppy classics, you'd be hard-pressed to do better.

Bermuda Bag
& Boat and Tote

In the 1980s era of preppy style, you couldn't beat a Bermuda bag. Typically round or oval in shape with a wooden handle, this most-reached-for style earned itself an honorable mention in *The Official Preppy Handbook*. It goes without saying that the deceptively spacious interior served a purpose: to keep everyday essentials close to hand. But let's not pretend that carrying cash, cards, and keys was all that the Bermuda bag did.

It was, and still is, loved for its chameleon-like ability to go with almost everything. The bag's defining feature—an interchangeable fabric cover—was made by brands like Lilly Pulitzer, Pappagallo, and DeLanthe in a variety of styles. From florals to bright colors, these covers were easy to button on and off. It's this versatility that makes it perfect for preps who prefer to stick faithfully to one style for daily use (rather than swapping contents from bag to bag) but still want their outfit and accessories to match. The finishing touch? Adding monogrammed initials, of course.

Speaking of monograms, L.L.Bean's Boat and Tote appeared in the summer of 1965 and was a hit for its durability and simplicity. It first came out in nautical red and blue that adhered to the New England seaside life, but the key selling points for consumers were the V-point closure on the underside and the "close." Soon enough, the product line grew with a range of colorways, sizes, and models (open or zip-top). And the sides were often embroidered with a preppy monogram or phrase. In its modern-day popularity, you can now find these canvas bags emblazoned with pop culture references or illustrations.

Blazer

Blazers are one of the most long-standing elements of preppy wardrobes, so it pays to know a thing or two about them. Traditionally, a blazer positions itself between a casual sports jacket and suit jacket. It is usually thigh-length and tends to be less structured around the shoulder and chest than more formal styles. Coming in different iterations, it can be double-breasted, single-buttoned, and made from a wide variety of fabrics—tweed, wool, and cotton included.

There's some dispute over the origins of this influential piece. One can be traced back to the mid-1800s, when sporting jackets in a bright shade of fire-like red (hence the term "blazer") were worn by the Cambridge rowing team. It's also said to reference the naval crew of HMS Blazer, who welcomed Queen Victoria onboard the ship wearing navy blue, double-breasted jackets in 1837. The name may even go back to the "blazes," or stripes that adorned the country club jackets in the 1870s. In any case, whether the blazer came from the high seas or sports fields, it transitioned from Britain into the American style lexicon via Ivy League universities.

From its revival in the swinging '60s as part of the mod movement to Giorgio Armani's unstructured designs in the 1970s that earned him the nickname King of the Blazer, it's proven to be a timeless piece that's resistant to passing trends. Paired with penny loafers and polos, blue hopsack iterations became a foundational piece in every prep-schoolboys' uniform.

Oxford Shirt

Oxford shirts are so ingrained in our wardrobes that it's hard to imagine a time when they didn't exist. After all, it's been an enduring piece for more than half a century—and for good reason. The Oxford shirt is defined by its signature fabric, which was one of four created by a Scottish textile mill with each named after a prestigious school. Oxford cloth was the only one that became a mainstay, largely down to its breathable cotton construction and distinctive basket-weave pattern.

The Oxford shirt was invented for polo players of the British Raj—a period when the British government directly ruled India—and usually, but not always, featured a button-down collar. Players used pins or buttons to stop their shirt collars from flapping in the wind as they raced around the field—a detail noticed by John E. Brooks, grandson of the founder of Brooks Brothers, during a visit to England in the late 1800s. Brooks brought his discovery back to America, and the brand's button-down shirt was born.

Worn by everyone from actors Paul Newman, James Dean, and Clark Gable to singer Taylor Swift, the Oxford shirt has a unique ability to evoke a simultaneously smart and casual look. It was cemented into culture thanks to the Ivy League set and has since achieved menswear (and womenswear) icon status. The Oxford shirt now comes in every color imaginable—from the original white to pale pink and light blue—and won't be going out of style any time soon.

Rugby Shirt

Many pieces in modern wardrobes originate from the world of sport, and the rugby shirt is no exception. This long-sleeved, collared shirt can be traced back to England in the late nineteenth century where it was adapted from early gentlemanly uniforms into a more athletic version that worked far better on the pitch.

Rugby shirts were made from ultra-thick cotton that was still breathable but wouldn't rip easily during play. The contrasting collar added a refined touch, while the low profile placket was made without buttons so it couldn't scrape a player's face. Distinctive horizontal bar stripes in various color combinations were added to help differentiate one team from another.

Alongside polos, rugby shirts are arguably one of the earliest concepts of athleisure. Rugby shirts found their way onto Ivy League campuses in the 1950s and became one of sportswear's greatest crossover hits. They were championed by brands such as Fred Perry, Gap, and Lacoste in the years that followed, and were subverted with a rock star spin by Mick Jagger—lead singer of The Rolling Stones—in the 1960s and '70s. Bright and bold rugby shirts emblazoned with "Coca-Cola" ruled the 1980s, British brand Hackett primed its return in the '90s, and American rapper Kanye West chose a blue and orange Ralph Lauren design to promote his debut record *The College Dropout* in 2004.

Tennis Skirt

The tennis skirt has been a design classic since the 1960s and continues to be a timeless piece. Typically worn above the knee, it consists of narrow folds or pleats created by sewing or pressing two parts of the fabric together. Alongside polos and collared dresses, the white tennis skirt taps into the country-club-chic that has long been associated with wealth, privilege, and of course, prep. Often paired with white socks with stripes, white sneakers, and sweaters casually slung over shoulders, it's now just as likely to be seen off the court as it is on the perfectly manicured lawns of the clubhouse.

Like many of the most tried-and-true preppy pieces, a pleated skirt also leans heavily into the scholarly aesthetic. Reminiscent of school uniforms, it's a look straight out the hallowed halls of an Ivy. Worn by *Gossip Girl*'s Blair Waldorf and the Upper East Side teenagers in the final scene of *Cruel Intentions*, a pleated skirt evokes core academia in all its glory.

Lilly Shift Dress

For a dress that was first worn to squeeze oranges, the "Lilly" has come a long way. The origin story of Lilly Pulitzer's Lilly shift dress is well-known in preppy circles. It goes back to 1959, when Lilly Pulitzer opened a juice stand in Palm Beach, Florida, using fruit from her husband's orchard. Lilly needed a vibrant, patterned design that would hide the juice stains that always used to cover her clothes after a day working, and so the now-iconic sleeveless shift dress was born.

They were an instant hit with Palm Beach's fashion set (former First Lady Jackie Kennedy included). Reimagined in everything from tropical palm leaves to bright florals, the Lilly has been a symbol of preppy resort wear ever since. The brand continues to sell thousands of the A-line dress each year in new prints that vary from jaguars set against a tropical palm leaf background to pink flamingos and bright florals.

Sweater Vest

The sweater vest made its debut in the very early twentieth century, when University of Michigan football players were given knitted tops for kit but customized them by removing the sleeves. Yet what started as a province for jocks, gained momentum around the Jazz Age—picture the monied, preppy style of the enigmatic Jay Gatsby in F. Scott Fitzgerald's classic *The Great Gatsby*. Since then, pop culture has often associated the sweater vest with grandads and geeks, whether that be the Weasley brothers from *Harry Potter*, Carlton Banks in *The Fresh Prince of Bel-Air*, or Chandler Bing from *Friends*.

The sweater vest embodies the sort of relaxed—but not scruffy—appeal that many are seeking from preppy staples. It wears just as easily with a button-up shirt as it does a T-shirt and, even better, is perfect for layering under a suit jacket or sport coat without adding unnecessary bulk.

Varsity Jacket

A varsity jacket—also known as the letterman—is one of the most instantly recognizable elements of a preppy wardrobe. While you may not need to be an Ivy Leaguer to wear one today, college students once had to earn the right to wear one by proving their athletic worth on the field.

The original style can be traced back to 1865 at Harvard's Cambridge, Massachusetts, campus—although it looked quite a bit different back then. Originally a thick-knitted sweater that players wore as uniforms, it was transformed by the Harvard baseball team into what's now known as the "letterman jacket" when a prominent "H" was sewn onto them. It's a look seen in *Grease*: Think Danny Zuko's cream Rydell cardigan emblazoned with a bold red "R."

Lettered jerseys were adopted a decade later by Harvard's football team before other colleges followed. From moving around its placement to changing the size, color, and font of the letter, each school's squad customized their letterman a little differently. Then the varsity jacket—with its wool body, contrasting leather sleeves, and giant letter on the side—was introduced in the 1930s when athletes needed something more substantial than a knit. As the mid-'60s Japanese photo book *Take Ivy* stated, "It is a must-have for every Ivy Leaguer."

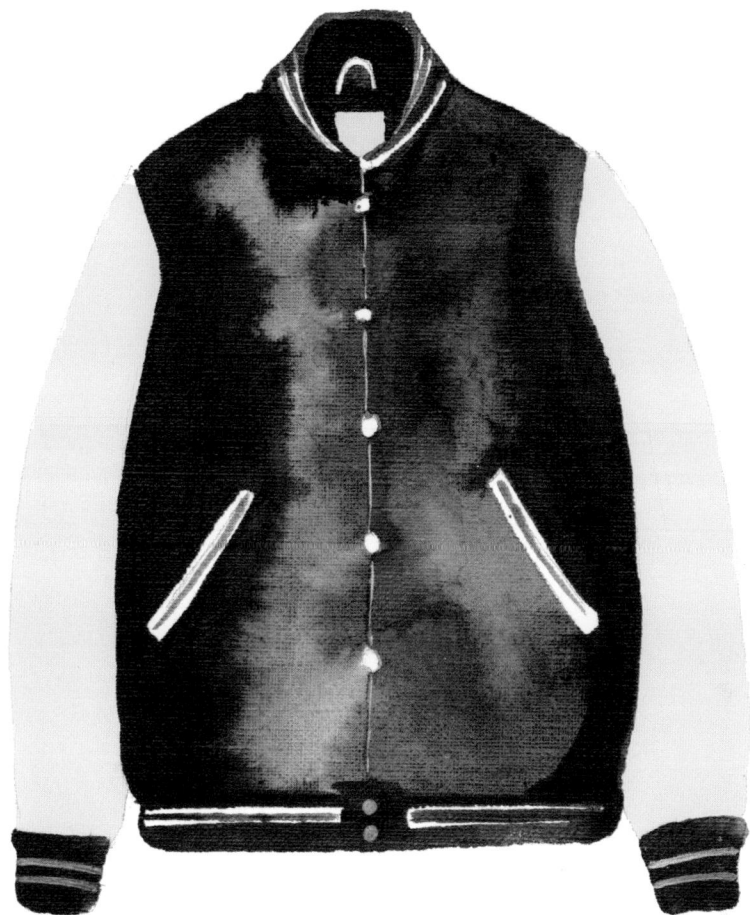

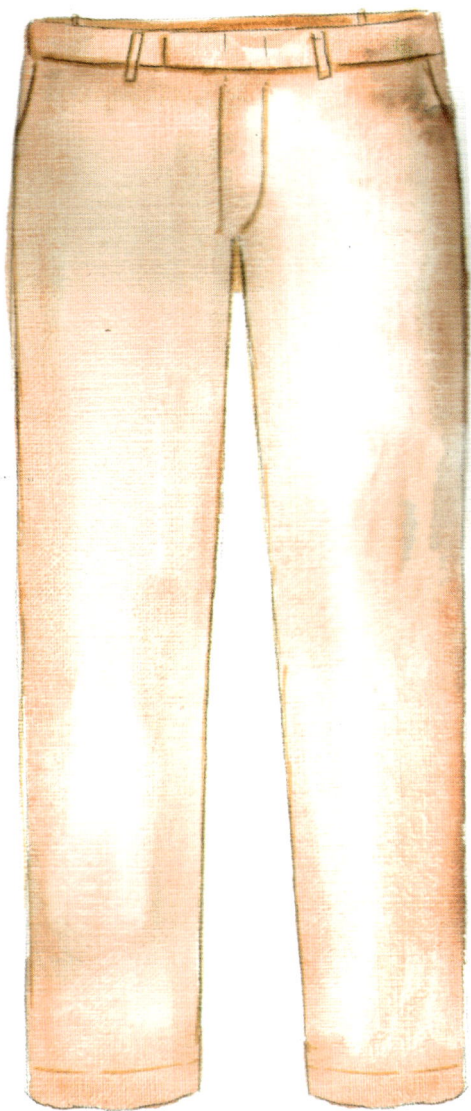

Chinos

When you think of the heyday of preppy style, chinos most certainly come to mind. After all, it was on the finest American campuses along the East Coast—where students wore them with insouciance—that chinos really came into their own alongside Oxford shirts and G.H. Bass & Co.'s Weejuns. Like so many other classics (bomber jackets, trench coats, and aviator sunglasses), they were originally intended for military kit bags before evolving into a civilian-life staple. The very first men's chinos came just after the Spanish-American War of 1898, when US troops stationed in the Philippines wore uniforms made from Chinese cotton twill. The name "chino" was taken from the Spanish word for China.

What made chinos so good at their job—their rugged durability, comfort, and versatility—is also what makes them popular today. They still include set-in pockets and a solid color with no fade lines, making them a touch smarter than jeans. Over the years, high-end designers and well-known brands alike have updated the menswear staple, subverting the proportions into more slimline silhouettes. Aside from every prep's favorite Nantucket Red hue, they've also been created in every shade imaginable. Yet, chinos remain so versatile that they've become a byword for goes-with-absolutely-anything.

Shaggy Dog Sweater

No discussion about preppy clothing would be complete without J. Press icon, the Shaggy Dog sweater. The brand has been offering the sweater for nearly eighty years, ever since Irving Press visited a knitting factory in Scotland. Still made in Scotland from pure Shetland wool and loved for its incredibly warm and fluffy feel, the Shaggy Dog sweater typically comes in a crew-neck style. It's since become a staple of traditional American menswear, having been worn by the likes of Cary Grant and JFK over the years.

It's also joined the ranks of many other authentic preppy pieces that have been reworked in new and entirely modern ways. The famous Shaggy Dog sweater was updated in 2018 in a collaboration between upstart label Rowing Blazers and J. Press. Not only was the sweater's signature tag moved to the left-hand side of the chest, it was also updated in a range of vibrant colors. You can forget Nantucket reds; the contemporary iterations came in everything from bright blue to orange to yellow—the bolder the better.

Chesterfield Coat

If you're looking for a coat that'll last an entire lifetime (only to be borrowed by your kids someday), head straight toward the most traditional and enduring of all: the Chesterfield. It's said to have been first worn by Englishman George Stanhope, the 6th Earl of Chesterfield, during the 1800s and has been on the back of distinguished—and preppy—men in the decades since.

The original design comes both single and double-breasted, featuring two pockets at the waist, one chest pocket, and a button front closure leading up to a traditionally velvet collar. While the basic silhouette has remained the same, the Chesterfield has gone through a few tweaks such as a slimmed-down fit and constructed from a range of different fabrics. Ideal for everyday wear, and appropriate over just about any outfit, this coat is as timeless as you'd expect.

Seersucker

Even though the fabric originated in Persia and India—its name derives from the Hindi word *sīrsakar* which translates as "milk and sugar"—seersucker has cultivated a distinctly American identity. Known for its ability to keep the wearer cool, the candy-striped fabric is typically made of a lightweight cotton and is woven in such a way that it has a puckered, crinkly texture. This helps it from sticking to the skin and lets air move more freely.

Legendary New Orleans haberdasher Joseph Haspel was one of the first in America to champion the breathable, low-maintenance, wrinkle-resistant nature of seersucker. Soon embraced by Louisiana laborers in the form of overalls, as a way to beat the heat, Haspel transitioned the fabric into men's tailored wardrobes with the launch of the seersucker suit in 1909. When Brooks Brothers in New York started selling seersucker suits in the 1920s, the style quickly became popularized with Ivy Leaguers and other high society men. And in 1933, when President Roosevelt attended a White House press conference, he wore his seersucker suit.

In 1962, the fabric was once again boomeranged into prominence by Gregory Peck when he played Atticus Finch in canon classic *To Kill a Mockingbird*, as well as the finely striped seersucker trunks sported by Dustin Hoffman in 1967's *The Graduate*. Whoever is your cinematic guide, what's important is the seersucker has become a byword for refined, warm-weather style. So much so, it now has its own national day.

Cable-Knit

Long before it was tossed over polos or tied around the shoulders of Ivy League students, cable-knit sweaters served a more functional purpose. They were originally worn by fishermen off the west coast of Ireland in the late 1800s. Prized for their unbeatable warmth and durability, cable-knit sweaters were traditionally knitted by wives and daughters to keep fishermen cozy and comfortable when they were out at sea. The distinctive braided stitch pattern at the front and sleeves provided extra insulation, as well as signifying the rope sailors used.

Later, it was brought into the mainstream by Elvis's blue high-neck version in the 1957 film *Jailhouse Rock*, while *Vogue* became one of the earliest fashion editorials to reference cable-knits in a 1958 article. Add into the mix Steve McQueen's classic cream sweater seen on John Lennon on holiday in the Scottish Highlands, Ryan O'Neal in *Love Story*, and Chris Evans in *Knives Out*. It becomes undeniable that this knit has transitioned from its hardy seafaring beginnings into an all-time classic.

Corduroy

Corduroy is plush, it's hardy, and thanks to its parallel ridges (or, to use the proper terminology, "wales"), it's also pretty warm. For the same reason, corduroy is just as tough as denim but feels softer and cozier. Its name originally comes from the French *corde du roi*, or the "cloth of kings," and has been the velvety fabric of choice of everyone from ancient Egyptians to aristocrats to the British working class.

First favored by students of ivy-covered institutions in the 1950s, it soon was being worn by musicians, artists, and creatives alike—think Mick Jagger of The Rolling Stones, Bob Dylan, Paul Newman, and Robert Redford—as a symbol of the antiestablishment movement in the '70s. Whether in the form of classic five-pocket tailored pants or as a single-button blazer, corduroy has endured for centuries. Its continuing relevance is a mark of its versatility, as well as its rugged, durable, and winter-proof appeal.

Stripes

Many patterns fall in and out of favor, but the majority associated with preppy style don't. Stripes—one of the oldest patterns in woven fabric—is one such stalwart. Featuring vertical or horizontal lines that can differ in spacing, thickness, and color, it's a classic pattern that's withstood decades of style changes.

One stripe synonymous with prep is the mighty Breton shirt. First worn by sailors in Brittany, France, to make them easier to spot out at sea, the nautical style was popularized by fashion designer Gabrielle "Coco" Chanel in 1917. These distinctive horizontal lines were then adopted by Ivy Leaguers, influenced by their penchant for yachts and sailing. Think preppy stripes and images of John F. Kennedy, Audrey Hepburn, Grace Kelly, and vintage Ralph Lauren and J.Crew advertisements abound. Breton, banker, or Bengal, there's a variation for everyone and rarely is there a dedicated follower of preppy style who does not own a stripe or three.

Checks

Always symmetrical, a check pattern consists of crossed horizontal and vertical lines that form evenly sized and spaced out tiles—picture the red-and-black blazer worn by Princess Diana in 1990, the pastel-pink sundress worn by Margot Robbie in *Barbie*, or Jackie Kennedy in yellow vintage Lilly Pulitzer.

Checks (especially gingham) have had a long-standing connection with preppy style. So much so, it was well-documented across students' shirts, blazers, shorts, and more in the cult *Take Ivy* photography book in 1965. Plus, the checkered pattern is so prevalent that it has gone beyond fashion and infiltrated preppy homes in the way of throws, quilts, pillows—you name it. Cementing its enduring appeal, the print has made a regular resurgence on fashion runways over the years. Luxury labels like Prada, Bottega Veneta, and Marc Jacobs continue to give checks a refined spin.

Plaid

It's no surprise that another pattern has made the list. After all, any true fan of preppy style is unlikely to shy away from throwing on a striking print or two. Designed with more than two colors (whereas checks only have two), plaid has a heritage that traces back several centuries to the tartan kilts worn by Scottish highlanders. It was then linked to British aristocracy, before plaids—especially brightly colored Madras plaid—began to be initiated into the world of "prep."

Plaid appeared on everything from blazers to pants to shirts to pleated skirts in the 1950s and '60s. And who could forget Kate Moss's plaid Bottega Veneta shacket and jeans combination at the brand's SS23 runway show? If you needed any further confirmation of plaid's prominence, it's also the pattern chosen to adorn the cover of Lisa Birnbach's *The Official Preppy Handbook*.

Argyle

A twist on tartan, this distinctive diamond pattern originates from the tartan of Clan Campbell of Argyll in western Scotland. Highlanders have been wearing it on socks and kilts since at least the seventeenth century, but it was knitwear brand Pringle of Scotland that took it mainstream in the 1920s. The design was adopted by the Duke of Windsor, who made it an immediately fashionable choice on and off the golf course.

As much as argyle is associated with British royalty, it found a place in the American preppy look. Argyle was sold to Ivy Leaguers by Brooks Brothers in the '50s, at both Harvard and Yale universities. By the 1990s, the character Cher Horowitz helped kick off a new wave of preppy minimalism with her monochrome argyle mini, white shirt, and black blazer combination. Since then, argyle has been worn by everyone from Kanye West to Madonna, and reinterpreted by brands such as Bottega Veneta, Prada, Dior, and Chanel.

Penny Loafers

When it comes to preppy footwear styles that have stood the test of time, the penny loafer is a great place to start. The shoe dates back to the 1920s, when similar styles were worn by Norwegian farmers and fishermen. When shoemaker G.H. Bass created its own version in 1936, it was marketed to wealthy, well-dressed men in *The New York Herald Tribune*. Called the "Weejun" loafer (derived from the word "Norwegian"), the brand's slip-on design quickly became a near-instant hit with students at America's elite colleges who were beginning to adopt a more casual style.

It was given the nickname "penny loafer" due to the Ivy League trend of putting a coin for the payphone into the shoe's front slot. The term has been popularized and still used today. The loafer and no-sock look also emerged on the same leafy college campuses, said to be attributed to the convenience when running late to class.

Boat Shoes

Much like the penny loafer, the boat shoe had a preppy reputation before it became a fixture in the world of fashion. But how did this lace-up make the leap from yacht deck to city street? One shoe lays claim to its origin story: Sperry.

It all started back in 1935, when Connecticut-based sailor Paul Sperry slipped and fell overboard his boat. Meanwhile, his cocker spaniel, Prince, was able to run around on snow and ice without losing traction. Inspired to create the world's first-ever nonslip boat shoe, the Top-Sider, he cut paw-like grooves into the rubber soles. By the end of the decade, they were worn by every member of the Cruising Club of America, and the US Navy had named it one of its standard issue shoes. It wasn't long before Sperry Top-Siders were then vaulted into popular culture, with the likes of President John F. Kennedy (complete with chinos and a gray sweater knotted around the shoulders) providing the springboard. Today, the silhouette continues to be reinvented with chunky lug soles, bold colors, and buckles to name a few—worn sockless, of course.

Rubber Moccasins

While the penny loafer and boat shoe are undoubtedly the most celebrated men's styles in a preppy shoe rack, the rubber moccasin also deserves a nod. It's been a symbol of functional style ever since L.L.Bean invented its signature model, the Bean Boot—also known as the Maine Hunting Shoe—in 1912. The brand's founder, Leon Leonwood Bean, noticed that his feet were getting wet and cold during hikes and hunting trips. He decided to combine the rubber soles of rain boots with the leather uppers of hunting boots. The boot then took the form of a more low-cut moccasin, which frequented the feet of college students in the 1980s, before surging in popularity again in the 2010s. So much so, shortages were widely reported, and L.L.Bean eventually had to ramp up its production to meet demand.

What truly sets the L.L.Bean moc apart—beyond its durable triple-needle stitching, rugged waterproof performance, and handsewn construction—is its ability to provide reliable traction in any weather. And as stated by *The Official Preppy Handbook*, "only Bean's has the true chain-tread outsole." As rugged and hardworking as they were over one hundred years ago, the rubber moccasin can, and should, be considered a thoroughly modern essential.

Wingtips

Maybe you're after shoes to wear with a suit to work, or perhaps with jeans at the weekend. Either way, if the dress code reads preppy, you're going to need a sturdy pair of wingtip shoes (a.k.a. brogues) at the center of your footwear arsenal.

Steeped in heritage, wingtips were originally made as a functional choice for Scottish and Irish farmers in the nineteenth century. A series of punched holes form a winglike "W" shape at the toe and once helped water drain from the shoes after trudging through wet, boggy terrain but is now purely decorative. There are, of course, many variations on the wingtip available to buy these days, but the key perforated detail remains the same. When expertly made from leather or suede, a good pair of wingtips can last a decade or more.

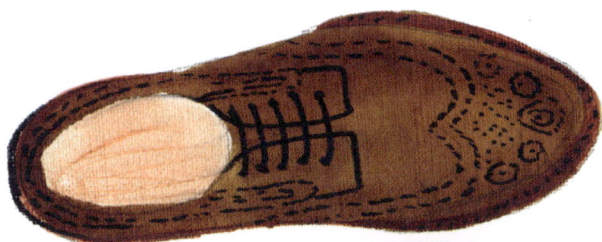

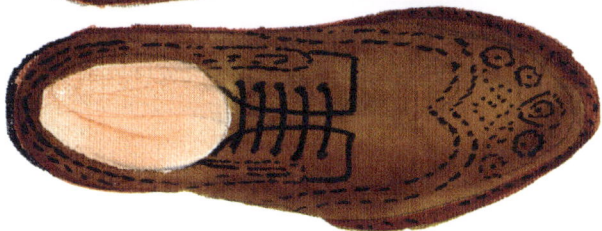

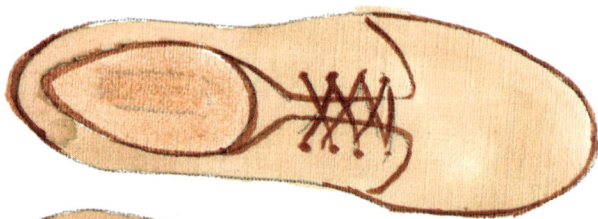

Bucks

Another pair of shoes that dominated the preppy footwear space in the 1950s, for men (and sometimes women), was the Buck. The style dates back nearly 150 years to 1870, where they were first made from deerskin hide (hence the "Bucks" nickname) before more commonly being constructed from suede. Characterized by a sturdy sole and an open lacing that separated them from the more formal Oxford, Bucks had a casual appeal that made them a popular choice on the golf course and tennis court.

It's said that it was the Duke of Windsor who propelled Bucks into the preppy fore, when he wore a white version on a trip to the East Coast in the 1920s. They were then advertised by brands like Roblee shoe company as offering "upper class comfort on campus." Of course, once they were in the preppy wardrobe, they needed to be styled a specific way. In the case of Bucks, it was the dirtier and the more beat up the better.

Mary Janes

A shoe that works just as well with a Diane von Furstenberg wrap dress on Madison Drive as it does paired with knee-length Bermuda shorts while summering in the Hamptons—Mary Janes are the obvious choice. Comfortable, versatile, and chic, they're imbued with a distinctive preppy flair. What defines the Mary Jane is the one (or more) single-buttoned strap across the top of the foot. The name comes from the shoes worn by Mary Jane, a character from Richard Outcault's *Buster Brown* comic strip in the early 1900s.

From Shirley Temple's white version in the 1934 film *Baby Take a Bow* to John Kennedy Jr. wearing a pair nearly thirty years later to his father's funeral, the style has consistent pop culture shout-outs. British fashion designer Mary Quant put model Twiggy in them in the '60s, and a resurgence of popularity in the '90s saw Cher walk around in chunky T-strap Mary Janes in *Clueless*, and also while Carrie searched for a Manolo Blahnik style in *Sex and the City*. Similar to preppy style as a whole, Mary Janes have evolved over time. More often than not, they're flat, but they've also been continually refreshed and revamped with a heel, platform, fabrics, and patterns.

Conclusion

Prep Forever

If there's one aesthetic that's lasted, it's prep. From being the easily recognized dress code of educated elites to hitting it big in the '80s, preppy style has had its hold on fashion for decades. In some ways, it's changed a lot over time, and yet in some instances, its evolution has been much more subtle. If there's one thing for certain, it's that today's prep is for everyone. Let's recap how the once exclusionary style has taken over the world in a way that no other look has.

Through the Decades

Preppy style started taking shape in the early 1900s, when wealthy students at the historic universities of America's East Coast (namely Princeton) flocked in droves to soon to be staples like penny loafers, Brooks Brothers button-downs, and sports blazers, styling them in new and entirely modern ways. Rugby shirts were enlivened with colorful stripes, collegiate sweatshirts paid homage to Ivy League colleges, and soft-shouldered jackets became the norm on and off campus. Wearing them came to signify your social standing. In the years that followed, it became a symbolic way for many of the prominent Black activists to counter racist preconceptions during the Civil Rights Movement, and then it was adopted by Japanese hipsters, initiated by the 1965 fashion photography book *Take Ivy*.

Prep was brought to life by Lilly Pulitzer's bold and bright vision and unintentionally rebranded by the film *Love Story*. Lisa Birnbach took it mainstream with her seminal satire *The Official Preppy Handbook*, with plenty of useful advice along with it on how to be a true prep. Suddenly, everyone was wearing it. Naturally, Ralph Lauren was there with his version of the American dream, giving reason for the Lo Lifes to ransack shops on Madison Avenue as well as providing the building blocks for Tommy Hilfiger's empire. Then came J.Crew, mass-marketing social aspiration through its glossy catalog and perfectly toeing the line between exclusivity and accessibility.

After the many pop culture moments in the early aughts that kept us captivated with prep, the aesthetic continued to make appearances on high-fashion runways (Miu Miu, Gucci, and Louis Vuitton to name a few). Teen retailers like Abercrombie & Fitch and Hollister worked their brand of prep Americana into every mall. In the late 2020s, Gen-Z's pursuit of nostalgia was the driving factor in preppy style filtering through social media—even if it was under popular hashtags like #oldmoney.

An Enduring Appeal

Ultimately, the enduring appeal of dressing preppy is quite simple. In an industry dominated by mass-produced, wear-it-once fashion that ends up in landfills, these are clothes you can really, truly live in. Prep is timeless, comfortable, well-made; a basic palette of style. The key pieces: the aforementioned polo shirts, cashmere crewnecks, and cable-knit sweaters are always going to be relevant. After all, it's a familiar style that's been around for more than half a century, one that adapts but never fades, like the foundation of American style. Basically, it's anything you'd imagine President John F. Kennedy to wear when sailing, or a dapper *Great Gatsby* character to show off down at the speakeasies, or Sidney Poitier's shirt-and-tie combinations to fill his wardrobe from the 1950s onwards.

Over time, the style has become so ubiquitous that many of the staple pieces are no longer discernible as being preppy at all. Oxford shirts and chinos that were once so synonymous with the privileged set, are now considered merely wardrobe essentials. There's a reason why today preppy style can be embraced by anyone; elements that were once so difficult to attain are more than likely in your wardrobe already—and that's what speaks to the beauty of it. Muffy Aldrich, editor of *Salt Water New England*, cites her reason for starting her infamous preppy blog over a decade ago as a way to "introduce new people to the pleasures and satisfactions of these classic clothes, which has only grown over time." The aesthetic has remained consistently stylish and, as much as anything can be, resistant to passing trends. And yet, it's one that is also constantly evolving.

Shifting Aspirations

"Preppy" carries all kinds of associations with exclusivity, rigidity, and wealth—or at least aspirations to it. It's deeply intertwined with the story of modern America; you can be whoever you want to be, as long as you dress the part. The rise in popularity of preppy home décor showed that it wasn't only about the clothes, but the emulation of the whole aspirational lifestyle. Decorating the home like a prep—throws knitted with the star-spangled banner, Polo Bear–embroidered cushions and plenty of tartan—provided another way to present affluence.

Initially based on class and the prestige of which Ivy League campus you attended, now there's plenty more to prep than its college campus and country-club reputation. The rules of a style that has long been considered restrictive have changed, opening the historically white, closed-off style to everyone. Recent iterations have lost a lot of the exclusionary aspects of the original, resulting in something that anyone can wear, style, and interpret as they wish. It now feels more about pointing out the problematic history behind the culture and welcoming those who have traditionally been excluded or forgotten.

When prep was regularly worn by President John F. Kennedy (a graduate of Harvard University), it signified being a part of the American elite. Donning the same narrow lapels, skinny ties, and soft-shouldered silhouettes created a sense of belonging to a clique that you wouldn't, or couldn't, otherwise be a part of. Now the preppy look implies little in terms of class. In fact, preppy has now shifted so much that when Michelle Obama was First Lady, she chose to wear J.Crew as a way to come across as more relatable and ordinary.

As the style filters through to younger generations, usually served up as social media content, these old standards of prep are twisted. Those seeing it through fresh eyes are looking to wear collegiate-inspired looks without the outdated notion of the clean-cut, class-indicating, and white-centric prep lifestyle. It's also about dressing with an element of irony; none of us are part of the elite, but we can still dress like we are. This new context recognizes prep's roots and pays homage to tradition but plays around with ideas and experiments. It's no longer taken seriously or seen as a measure of status or class of whoever is wearing it.

The fact that preppy style was born out of rebellion, evolved into conformity, and then circled back into rebellion is often overlooked. Early prep's subversive side has been minimized by the stereotypically uptight prep that became popular on the back of the 1980's *Handbook*. When students were photographed for *Take Ivy* in the 1960s, it was revolutionary style icons that the photographers found—in loafers without socks and baggy chinos—instead of the conformist prepsters they had expected. Once the style had been adopted by the

Miyuki Tribe in Japan, the group of young men were viewed as delinquents for going against the norm by wearing Ivy League–inspired blue blazers and Bermuda shorts. Even during the Civil Rights Movement, activists such as Dr. Martin Luther King Jr. were wearing repp ties, fitted blazers, and seersucker jackets as they protested. It proves, in contrast to popular opinion, that being preppy is not always about fitting in.

Wear It Your Way

Preppy may go quiet for periods, overshadowed at points by fleeting aesthetics and trends like grunge or punk, but it always comes back. However, it never looks exactly the same. Of course, a lot of this comes down to the styling, which is an equally important element of the preppy aesthetic—styling is at the center of the look. With preppy, it's not enough to choose all the right preppy pieces. They have to be worn in a way that's fashionable too. On campus, it was about taking a nonchalant approach. To look good without it looking like you were trying. Then it became about following the rules laid out in the handbook. The Lo Lifes styled them differently, taking a more-is-more approach in order to get noticed. In the late 2020s, shrunken polo shirts dominated, pleated skirts had to be mid length, and loafers needed to be chunky. The aspect of styling preppy staples is one that is always shifting.

Preppy style is now less about being an unofficial uniform and more about individuality, choosing pieces that nod to this traditional way of dress but applying them to your personal style. Despite its classic nature, it's surprisingly easy to put your own spin on preppy style. Appropriated by the likes of Princess Diana and Jackie Onassis, to Snoop Dogg and Tyler, the Creator, there's some aspect of the aesthetic that everyone can make their own. It proves prep *is* always cool. It's just about how you wear it.

We're All Preppy Now

Whether you know it as "Ivy style," "stealth wealth," "old money aesthetic," or any of the other trends ending with "-core," it all comes back to preppy. The name may have changed over the course of the past one hundred years, but it's the same aesthetic that's left an indelible impression on the way we dress. No longer a look reserved for the elite, the version of prep that persists is worn by people who would never describe themselves as preps or who have never set foot on an Ivy League campus. It's transcended its social origins to symbolize understated elegance and wealth without the need to try too hard.

Whether it's used as an opportunity to challenge the original values (over and over and over again) or just as a nice way to dress and feel more put together, prep will always be a feature in our wardrobes in one way or another. Preppy comes and goes but also never leaves. It has a unique ability to grow and evolve, while still maintaining the timelessness that makes the aesthetic so fun to tap into. It's the very reason why preppy style is still going strong after more than a century. Prep lasts.

Acknowledgments

My sincere appreciation goes to Nicole James for giving me the opportunity to write this book and for trusting me to get it over the finish line. Also to my editor, Katey Abraham, whose guidance, expertise, and endless patience made it what it is.

I want to say thank you to Simon Dance, who many, many years ago gifted me Sheryl Sandberg's *Lean In* to read and who (unknowingly) inspired me to try to achieve success both at work and at home.

Special thanks to my children. Isabella and Autumn, I'm sorry for the rushed bedtimes, extra screen time, and for being the cause behind the often asked—yet somehow always enthusiastic—question, "Is it finished yet?"

I couldn't have got it done without my mother Marian Dixon's constant support (babysitting duties and food deliveries included) and to my father, Terry Gomersall, who taught me all about hard work, and who I only wish could be here to read it.

Lastly, I'm forever grateful for those who put up with me after late nights, early mornings, and seeing only my forehead behind a laptop for months; you know who you are.

About the Author

Rosalyn Gomersall is a writer born and raised in Hertfordshire, UK. She has a bachelor's degree in journalism from London's City University and has spent over a decade writing about fashion for a variety of luxury brands. *Preppy Style* is her first book.

First published in 2025 by Rock Point, an imprint of The Quarto Group,
142 West 36th Street, 4th Floor, New York, NY 10018, USA
(212) 779-4972 www.Quarto.com

EEA Representation, WTS Tax d.o.o.,
Žanova ulica 3, 4000 Kranj, Slovenia.
www.wts-tax.si

Rock Point titles are also available at discount for retail, wholesale, promotional, and bulk purchase. For details, contact the Special Sales Manager by email at specialsales@quarto.com or by mail at The Quarto Group, Attn: Special Sales Manager, 100 Cummings Center Suite 265D, Beverly, MA 01915 USA.

10 9 8 7 6 5 4 3 2 1

ISBN: 978-1-57715-546-1

Digital edition published in 2025
eISBN: 978-0-76039-757-2

Library of Congress Cataloging-in-Publication Data

Names: Gomersall, Rosalyn, author.
Title: Preppy style : a modern guide to timeless fashion / Rosalyn Gomersall.
Description: New York : Rock Point, 2025. | Summary: "Full of nostalgic and
    inspirational illustrations, Preppy Style provides a historical overview
    of prep culture, from iconic looks to the newest preppy trends"--
    Provided by publisher.
Identifiers: LCCN 2025009969 (print) | LCCN 2025009970 (ebook) | ISBN
    9781577155461 (print) | ISBN 9780760397572 (ebook)
Subjects: LCSH: Clothing and dress--Social aspects--United States--History.
    | Preppies.
Classification: LCC GT605 .G66 2025 (print) | LCC GT605 (ebook) | DDC
    391.00973--dc23/eng/20250508
LC record available at https://lccn.loc.gov/2025009969
LC ebook record available at https://lccn.loc.gov/2025009970

Group Publisher: Rage Kindelsperger
Editorial Director: Erin Canning
Creative Director: Laura Drew
Managing Editor: Cara Donaldson
Senior Acquiring Editor: Nicole James
Editor: Katelynn Abraham
Cover and Interior Design: Evelin Kasikov
Illustrations: Jessica Durrant

Printed in Huizhou, Guangdong, China TT072025